Fi

S UNIVERSITY COLLEGE

For all my mothers.

# FLOWERS OF THE
# FAIREST

ROSEMARY CONRY

**Brandon Original Paperback**

Published in 2002
by Brandon
an imprint of Mount Eagle Publications,
Dingle, Co. Kerry, Ireland

ISBN 0 86322 303 6

Cover design by Anú Design
Typeset by Red Barn Publishing, Skibbereen
Printed by Mackays of Chatham Ltd


www.brandonbooks.com

# Contents

# INTRODUCTION

*Bring flowers of the fairest, bring blossoms the rarest*
*From garden and woodland and hillside and dale.*
*Our full hearts are swelling – our glad voices telling*
*The praise of the loveliest flower of the vale.*

CAPPAGH HOSPITAL LAY some way to the north-west of Dublin city, on the edge of a village called Finglas. In 1940, when I went there as a patient, the war was well under way and very few cars were seen on the roads. Buses, too, were infrequent but on Sundays and Wednesdays, the only visiting days, an extra bus was laid on, and instead of ending its journey at the terminus outside Finglas church, it drove the extra half mile or so to the hospital gates. The patients at Cappagh were children whose bones were infected by a form of tuberculosis, caused by drinking milk from the carrier cows. In my childhood, the milkman came to our house twice a day to fill our jugs with milk that was frothy and often still warm from the udder. I drank the rich, creamy liquid at every meal, encouraged by my mother who never for a moment doubted that milk was the fount of all nourishment, especially at a time when other foods were in short supply.

Thus, we children of Cappagh were, in the main, victims of that form of the disease which attacked the bones and joints and, although spared the dreaded, consumptive variety that so often killed, many of us spent years

7

confined to bed, strapped on to padded iron frames which held us in fixed positions, according to where we were affected. We lay in the open air, waiting for the disease to burn itself out, then had to learn to use our limbs again or, more likely, to adapt our movements to the constrictions of a fused, useless joint.

We were cared for, with a strict kind of devotion, by the Irish Sisters of Charity, who trained girls of ability to be nurses of the highest order. After serving their time, some nurses went on to become nuns themselves. Others were only too pleased to take a chance on marriage – if it was offered – but whatever they did after leaving Cappagh, the mention of its name gave them credit and respect, wherever they found themselves.

We lived under glass-roofed verandas night and day, winter and summer – all, that is but the patients who were gravely ill and needed watching. When driving rain and snow made it impossible to keep the beds dry, we were drawn back into the wards and tall, folding doors were pulled across to keep us sheltered until the storm was over.

I remember, perhaps unreliably, the names of those among whom I lay for more than two years. In any case, I have given them new ones so as not to make wrong attributions. Faces I can see more clearly, and out of my store of indelible memories I have woven this account of childhood, as experienced by three real girls: Eileen, Pauline and myself, Rosemary, always in the middle.

Nuns, nurses, doctors and teachers are clear in my mind, their words and actions and the cruelty and unfairness to which we had no right of reply. Such as these were, I bear our keepers no ill will, for the times were austere for everyone and we children were not meant to know that adults were only human.

*Introduction*

I have put remembered phrases into our mouths as I see fit and taken some liberties in describing events which some, with longer memories, might question. But I can vouch for the sights and sounds, the taste, smell and feel of those times that are long gone but which I, like a latter-day ancient mariner, feel compelled to relate.

# EARLY DAYS

WE STARTED OUR lives as English children, my brother Paul and I, coming with our parents to live in Sandycove when I was four years old and my brother nine. For my father, it meant promotion to a small outpost of the London-based firm which employed him. Having left Ireland as a young man to fight in the First World War, he was, after small beginnings in civilian life, returning with jubilation to his Dublin roots to be the managing director of the Irish branch of the company.

We would have a wonderful life in Ireland, my mother confidently predicted, with the added pleasure for her of living near her own brother, who was a prominent Dublin businessman and lived in a rich man's house.

My mother was very pretty and she dressed, someone once said, with 'the languid elegance of a duchess'. She set out to be a great asset to her husband by making a big impact on social occasions in the clubs and societies which he would, in his new position, be urged to join. But in her heart, she found it hard to settle. Although completely Irish, she had lived in England for most of her life, and in almost every way that mattered to her, she found Dublin sadly wanting. For her, the only place to live was London, in Chelsea or Knightsbridge, and she spoke of these places with sighs of unfulfilled desire.

Our home was a semi-detached villa on a leafy avenue which ran downhill from the tramlines to the seafront. The perfect place to live, she would outwardly agree with her contented neighbours, with its fresh sea air and marvellous views. But the glamorous life she craved seldom materialised, and so the move to Ireland remained always, for her, a backward step.

For me, life in Sandycove was full of interest. When the weather was warm, I learned to swim in the sandy harbour with a rubber ring around my chest, and when the water was too cold for swimming, I climbed over the rocks with my brother and, with a bent pin attached to a length of twine, fished in pools for stingoes. In the winter, I went to a dancing class and began to learn the piano from a Protestant lady who ran a little music school on our avenue.

I had a keen ear for music and the accents of the local people and was, even at such an early age, a good mimic. My parents were amused by my skill but took great care to ensure that no Irish expressions, picked up from the common people, crept into my everyday speech. I became known as a charming, if slightly forward child, who called her mother 'Mummy', said 'shall' and 'shan't' instead of 'will' and 'won't' and was able to speak well to grown-ups and even sing a song when asked.

With no road to cross, I was soon allowed to run messages to the nearby shops, with money wrapped up in the shopping list, and I was never afraid to start a conversation with anyone who was willing to respond.

At the age of six, I was sent to St Anne's preparatory school, a twenty-minute walk from home. I was soon considered sensible enough to make the journey on my own, and so I stepped proudly into the wider world in my smart uniform with a stiff leather satchel on my back. I was placed at once in the first Communion class, and thus together with the joys of new friends and new books, I became interested in Jesus, who, I was told, would soon enter my heart and stay with me for ever.

In the afternoons, while Mummy rested on the sofa with her feet up, I squatted on the hearthrug and earnestly related every detail of my discoveries. I was full of wondering, too, about the different ways of life I saw as I passed through the area called Glasthule, where poor people lived. Some were so poor, I told her, that the children had no shoes and their mothers wore black shawls instead of coats. Mummy said it was sweet of me to worry, but it would be simply impossible to make everyone rich and happy. We just had to accept things the way they were. 'Such is life,' she would say.

By listening to Mummy, I learned that the people who lived in corporation cottages might not be well off but they were, on the whole, decent and hard-working. Great credit was due to some of them, she said, for the way they kept their little houses so clean and turned out their children immaculately for mass on Sundays, with all those shoes polished and the little girls' hair done up in ringlets that must have taken hours of fiddling to achieve.

On the other hand, the people who lived in the tenement buildings were a different matter altogether. They were really, really poor and hardly able to put on a show at all, for as well as having no money, they had no bathrooms or even a boiler for heating up water.

I was always a bit nervous when I had to pass the Buildings – and it would have been hard to avoid them, as they stood between our house and all the places I had to get to. On my way to and from school, I took to walking by as fast as I could, on the opposite side of the road, to keep as far away as possible from the really poor children, for I soon learned that they had no time for the likes of me.

The Buildings consisted of two oblong blocks of red brick, facing each other across a concrete area and connected by a cat's cradle of clothesline, on which the really poor hung their sorry garments out to dry. The one-roomed dwellings were on two tiers, each one having a small window and a door, opening on to an iron-railed passage. The upper floor was reached by metal staircases at each end, which clanged and echoed constantly under the heavy pounding of boots and bare feet.

Hundreds of children lived in the Buildings. It seemed to me that they all screeched together as they played hopscotch, swung on flittered ropes hanging from lamp-posts or ferociously kicked balls across the area. I wondered where those children slept, whether they had a place to sit down and eat their dinner, if there was room for a table at all in those chicken-coop homes. Or were the thick doorsteps of bread I would see them eating in the street all they ever got to eat? Just the look of them was enough to make me thankful to be living in a nice, quiet avenue, in a semi-detached house with a garden and a bedroom of my own.

Mrs Berry lived in the Buildings and she had no teeth. Once a week she came to scrub our kitchen floor and put blacklead on the range. When the schools broke up for the holidays, she brought one of her five daughters with her, always the same daughter, who was called Titchy but whose real name, she told me in a cheeky, put-on accent, was Marie Therese.

'She does be fightin' with the others, ma'am,' Mrs Berry apologised. Mummy said kindly that it was quite all right and that Titchy could play in the garden.

There was a smell off Titchy which came, I supposed, from washing herself in cold water and she had sores on her face. Her nose was always running, and I never once saw her with a handkerchief. On the very first morning she came to our house, she poked her tongue out at me and said, 'I don't like you, young one,' which hurt my feelings so badly that I lost all pity for her poverty. I was kind to her, of course, for we were taught in school never to look down on the poor, because God loved them best of all and had compassion on them. Besides, I was afraid to be nasty to Titchy, in case I might meet her sometime along the seafront with her gang when, without her mother to keep her in order, she might egg them on to throw stones or skim a slate from the beach towards my legs. As long as she was in our garden, though, Titchy had nothing much to say for herself but stared with her mouth open at everything from the lawnmower to the shoes on my feet.

'You can ride my tricycle, if you like,' I told her, and I gave her heaps of Marie biscuits out of the tin in the kitchen. Titchy scoffed the biscuits without a word of thanks and sat glued to the saddle of my tricycle all morning, riding round and round in circles, gouging lumps out of the lawn, for which I later got the blame. After she had gone, I wiped the saddle with a cloth sprinkled with Vim.

Mrs Berry's husband was away serving in the British army, and Mummy said she hoped he was sending money home for the children. Mrs Berry threw back her head and laughed, showing her salmon-pink gums, and said God only knew how she was able to put food in their mouths at all.

'How much money would Mrs Berry get every week?' I asked Mummy in the tram on our way home from the shops. She said, 'About a pound, or twenty-five bob, I suppose.'

Then I asked the price of every single thing in our shopping basket and it added up to two pounds, three shillings and fourpence ha'penny. Mummy agreed that it was a terrible thing to be as poor as Mrs Berry.

And yet Mrs Berry was fat, bulging softly out of her wrap-over pinny. Our neighbour Mrs Bower said it was shocking how quickly the poor soul had aged, as it seemed like only yesterday that she was a young slip of a girl, pretty and blonde and doing a line with Findlaters' messenger boy. It was hard to imagine.

When Mrs Berry got her silver money at the end of the morning, she smiled her thanks and said Mummy was very good to her. Two half-crowns were her wages, and she got an extra florin for the pound of butter which Mummy bought from her every week. Mummy said the worst thing about the war for her was the butter rationing. 'Not being able to spread it on thick is a real hardship for me,' she said. Mrs Berry caught on quick and was only too pleased to do a deal.

The three coins went into the pocket over her stomach, where she kept patting them with her red hands as she wiped down a few more tops and door handles, to show that she was giving good value for her wage. Then she roared for Titchy to 'Come on home,' and waddled off on her down-at-heel shoes.

'Does Mrs Berry not like butter,' I asked Mummy during the afternoon rest.

'She'd rather have the money.'

'What would her children eat on their bread, then?'

'I don't know – dripping, or that awful cheap jam that has no real fruit in it.'

'Would they ever have rashers and eggs or roast beef?'

'Maybe, sometimes, at Christmas.' Mummy's eyes began to droop.

'Could we not give Mrs Berry more money, so she wouldn't have to sell her butter ration?'

'Don't be silly,' Mummy said sharply. 'I'm not made of money, you know.'

'But we are rich, are we not?'

'Oh, I wouldn't say that.'

'Not as rich as Uncle Dick, but richer than Mrs Berry.'

'I suppose you're right,' Mummy sighed.

'Much, much richer.'

'Hmmm.'

'Mummy, don't go to sleep when I'm talking to you!'

'I'm not sleeping, darling, I'm just resting my eyes.'

'Can I give Titchy my old clothes?'

'We'll see. Don't worry me now.'

Mrs Bower, who was a nurse before she was married, said that what Titchy had on

her face was impetigo and that I should not be allowed to play with her because it was highly contagious. From then on, whenever Titchy came, the tricycle stayed locked in the shed and I sat quietly in my bedroom, reading my books or trying, with not much joy, to correct the holes in my knitting without having to rip it all out.

I was not sorry to be kept away from Titchy, but I felt even more nervous about having to pass the Buildings in future, for fear she would come after me in earnest and beat me up for being rich. I tried to put her out of my mind, but knowing that she was down in the garden for the whole morning with nothing to do and no one to play with, I couldn't resist, every now and then, creeping over to the window and peeping over the sill to see what she was up to. Mostly, she was just leaning against the kitchen doorframe, doing nothing at all, only watching her mother at work and chewing on the lapel of her coat.

Mrs Bower was the first to notice that I was limping. She took a special interest in our family and watched our comings and goings. Regarding my mother, I imagine, as being a bit on the flighty side, she was always ready with a word or two of advice.

'I noticed the limp,' she said one day in a casual way, as if my mother was sure to have noticed it, too.

Mummy would have none of it. She complained all the time that Mrs Bower was nosy and overfamiliar and did all she could to keep her at a distance. Not that Mrs Bower minded, or even noticed. She was inclined to borrow 'drops of milk' or 'pinches of sugar' as an excuse to start a chat. There would be a knock at the front door, and when it was opened, a jug or bowl would appear over the low wall between our two front doors, closely followed by Mrs Bower's big round face, full of sincerity and bursting to say what was on her mind.

On the subject of the limp my mother replied shortly, 'It's nothing. We don't make a fuss.'

A while later it was, 'That child is in pain.'

'Growing pains,' my mother conceded.

Mrs Bower said she was a great believer in Parrish's Food. 'It has iron in it,' she said.

In the corner shop at the top of the avenue, where I went to spend my pocket money, Miss Mac came out from behind the counter and took a scissors to the elastic in the leg of my knickers. 'It's no wonder you've been limping,' she said. 'That elastic was stopping your circulation.'

My mother was relieved to latch on to so simple a solution to the problem. She bought me some new knickers and a bottle of the sweet, red linctus called Parrish's Food, which I quite enjoyed, although it did nothing to relieve the pain in my leg, which grew worse by the day.

In school my teacher said, 'Don't slouch. Ladies must have good deportment.' I explained about the growing pains, but she only laughed and said there was no such thing and where had I heard such nonsense? One day she sent me home with a note.

My walk home took longer than ever before. I had to ease myself along by clinging to garden walls and gates and cross the side roads in hops and skips. Twice I fell over and, picking myself up, stood still for a while to brush the dust off my coat and stare back at the road, as though I had been tripped up by some obstruction.

The Buildings were quiet enough at that time of day, but instead there was the National School to be got past. It was playtime and the forecourt was teeming with chattering children skipping and chanting:

> *Stands the lady on the mountain, who she is I do not know.*
> *All she wants is gold and silver, into the circle you must go!*

On spotting my private school uniform, they abandoned their games and swarmed like bees all over the tall railings to watch my progress. Hands appeared everywhere on the bars, deliberately blocking my attempts to reach for a hold.

'Ay, young one, wha's wrong witcher leg?'

'Growing pains.'

'Graowing pains? Ow, wot a shime!' Insolent eyes shifted downwards to stare at my feet, and when at last I had passed out of sight, I was followed by catcalls.

'Peggy's leg!'

'Hoppalong Cassidy!'

'Where's yer horse?'

A bell rang and the children suddenly scattered. A harsh-voiced teacher called them into ranks, and moments later the playground was empty and silent.

After that, there were only the trams to worry about. They hurtled along the main road at alarming speed, their rods spitting sparks as they clashed with the overhead wires, lurching wildly as the tracks followed the bend in the road at the spot where I had to cross over. The drivers stamped on their footbells to give warning of their approach, but you still had to be quick about it. Little Billy Patrick, with the golden curls, had been run over and killed here, and his mother had never stopped crying since. My mother stepped into shop doorways when she saw Mrs Patrick coming towards her, saying she was a real misery, but later would admit, 'Ah, but it's a terrible thing to lose a child. You'd never get over that.'

'Always ask a nice lady to see you across the road,' she instructed me, but on that day I saw no one except two red-faced men coming out of Farrell's pub.

'Excuse me, please . . . but I can't walk. ' They grinned as I politely said my piece, but when they realised that I could go no further on my own, they sat me up on their interlocked hands, swept me across the road in a 'Carry the Lady to London' and down the avenue to my doorstep, where Mummy greeted us with a white face.

'My leg jumps at every small noise,' I told the doctor, whose name was Jack Frost, 'even at the rustle of a newspaper.' He took my hand and said I was a very brave girl. 'I'm going to send you to see a big shot in Dublin,' he said in a hearty voice that made me feel I had a rare treat in store. 'Harry Macauley is the best orthopaedic man in the country.'

I went with my parents in a taxi to a city hospital where x-rays were taken and after that to a tall, sombre house in Fitzwilliam Square where, I was told, all the big shots had their consulting rooms. You could see your face in the brasses on the front door, and in the dark hall a man-sized clock solemnly ticked away the seconds.

Mr Macauley examined the negatives of my hip and laid his hand precisely on my pain. 'She will have to go to Cappagh,' he told my parents, 'as soon as Sister Finbar has a bed for her.'

At home again, I lay in the privileged comfort of my parents' bed to await the ambulance. Propped up on a mountain of pillows, I drank warm milk and dipped fingers of bread into a new-laid egg. I liked the sound of the name 'Cappagh', thought it would be great not to have to walk to school for a while, and I revelled in the unusual attention that was being showered upon me.

When my brother came home from school, he sat beside my bed and read to me from Grimms' fairy tales. My favourite story was 'The Twelve Dancing Princesses', and I made him read it twice.

# A New Life

I ARRIVED IN Cappagh by ambulance one day in the early spring, soon after my seventh birthday. A nurse was waiting for me in the front hall. I was put lying on a trolley and wheeled down long corridors to a ward called Blessed Imelda's. There I was taken in hand by two more nurses and put to bed, while my parents were steered in another direction to be interviewed by Sister Finbar. From the back of the empty ward, I looked with growing apprehension at the rows of beds outside on the veranda and tried to hold on to the fast-fading belief that I would, as Mummy kept saying, be back at home 'in no time at all'. They changed me into a uniform gown of blue and white gingham, bandaged my quivering leg and raised it up on a contraption they called 'a weight and pulley', which, as if by magic, stopped my pain. Then, as the nurses tightly tucked in my bedclothes, chatting to me cheerfully as if there was no reason in the world to be worried, I knew for sure that there was no escape. I had become a patient.

Sister Finbar returned with my parents and called for chairs to be brought. She, too, was smiling broadly, as if all the news was good. 'Isn't that better now?' she said with satisfaction.

My mother's face puckered at the sight of me. 'How long, please, how long?' she pleaded.

'Not long,' said the nun. 'You are not to worry now.

She is in good hands.'

My mother's shoulders began to shake and she covered her face with her hands. Sister Finbar took her by the arm and led her out to the corridor. 'Not in front of the child,' I heard her say.

My father stayed a while longer. 'Be a soldier,' he said. 'Show them what you are made of!'

After my parents left, I was wheeled out to take my place on the veranda. 'You will soon settle in', said Sister Finbar, 'and make new friends.'

'Never!' I thought miserably. I did not like the look of these girls at all. They had the look of the National School about them and gawked at me with open mouths. I was sure that I would get nothing but abuse from them, and in their disabilities many of them were hard to look at. I kept my eyes on the sky.

I could not think of anything suitable to say to Sister Finbar, who stood over me watching and waiting for my reactions to my new surroundings. I held back my tears and managed a smile, just wishing she would go away.

'Look,' she said, 'wave to your Mammy and Daddy.' She pointed across the open space towards the gate, where I could see my mother fluttering her hands and my father waving his hat in the air.

'I call her Mummy,' I murmured, but she did not seem to hear.

I wanted to scream and shout, 'Please don't leave me in this horrible place. My pain has gone away and I hate everyone here!' But with so many eyes fixed on me, I was afraid to show weakness. I raised myself awkwardly on one elbow and waved to my parents in a cheery way, just as I did on most evenings from my perch on our gatepost at home as my father turned into the avenue on his return home from the office.

'Now,' said Sister Finbar when my parents had disappeared from view, 'I've put you beside Pauline, who is the same age as yourself. Won't you be good to Rosemary, Pauline, and help her to settle?' She drew our beds together as she spoke and left us, promising to return when she had a spare minute, with a little treat for the two of us.

'Don't worry, Sister. I'll mind her for you.'

The girl in the next bed was thin as a stick and pure white. Not a spot of pinkness showed in her cheeks, only a few pale freckles, like splashes of milky tea, were scattered across her nose. She lay crooked in her bed as though she had been dropped on it from the sky. The hands that lay crossed over her chest were badly twisted, and she had some difficulty in turning her head. Her blue eyes seemed too big for her face, and she spoke in a gentle, comforting voice, as though her own crippled state gave her the right to teach others how to cope with theirs.

'Don't be frettin' now,' she said. 'You'll be grand here, and, please God, your mammy will be out to see you on Sunday.'

But kind words were wasted on me. There was no comfort in thinking of the three, no four days until Sunday, and I hated her for telling me what I did not want to hear. I wished I could stop her voice, push her bed away. Hit her! I told myself that she didn't know what she was talking about, for wasn't she a terrible cripple, while all I had was a pain in my leg and that would be cured in no time. No time at all.

'Will your mother – mammy – be here on Sunday?' I asked, to show politeness and put a stop to her sympathy.

She laughed. 'Not at all. Sure, I'm an orphan. Sometimes priests do come, or ordinary people who are just visiting the hospital. Sister Finbar always brings them to my bed because I have no visitors of my own. They're all very good. One time, Sister Ann came with Breege-God-help-her from the orphanage. I was only delighted to see them. Breege-God-help-her was going to cousins in England. They found work for her in a laundry because she was so good at the ironing. Oh, the excitement of it! She was beside herself!'

'How long have you been here?' I asked, trying not to look at her hands.

'Seven months exactly,' she said. 'It was the Feast of the Assumption when I came, and this year, please God, I'll be making my first Holy Communion on that very day. Have you made yours yet?'

I shook my head. 'Well, then, we'll be making ours together in August. Sister Patrick comes of a Tuesday, to prepare us. She's lovely, Sister Patrick. She'll give you holy pictures.'

'But I'll be at home by then,' I insisted. 'I am in the first Communion class at my school.'

'So you will, please God,' said Pauline, 'an' I'll be getting' up out of the bed soon now. I've only to be measured for callipers and a corset, and when I get them, I'll be able to walk.' Her face was lit by the happy thought and she added another 'please God'.

Other children called out, demanding to know my name, what age I was and what I had wrong with me. I answered some but not others with short words, and they were silenced for the moment by my different way of talking. But even though I did not look at them, I could feel their watchful, curious eyes on me for the rest of the day.

By the evening, when the last prayers were said and the beds pulled back under the glass roof of the veranda, it seemed that I had been listening to Pauline for hours.

At teatime we had eaten bread and jam from the same plate and shared between us the handful of sweets which Sister Finbar dug out of her apron pocket.

I was relieved when the nurses pulled our beds apart, for the only thing I wanted in all the world was to go to sleep and wake up in my own bed to find that all this was only a bad dream.

Still Pauline went on talking, and in the fading light, across the space between our beds, she told me all about life in the orphanage.

'I don't remember my parents at all. They died when I was a baby, and after that I lived in the orphanage. I had things wrong with me from the start, but I managed all right until last year, when I was six years old. Sister Ursula, she was the reverend mother, said I couldn't stay there any longer but would have to go to hospital for the treatment and the schoolin'.'

'"Please God, you will be much improved," she said, "and then, of course, you can come back to visit us." She was good to me that day, I remember, and that was unusual for she was strict – oh, very strict! But it was only for our own good. I was afraid and lonely to be leavin', but now I like here better than the orphanage. Sister Finbar is the best mother anyone could have.

'My real mother? No, I don't know what happened her. She died young and in the state of grace. That's all I know, and sure you don't miss what you've never had, isn't that right?

'It was only things that were said sometimes that would make me feel kind of afraid. Like when Breege-God-help-her was havin' one of her noisy days and shoutin' out mad things. Oh, she was a holy terror! She worked in the kitchen, helpin' Sister Margaret Mary with the cookin', and when she was on her best behaviour, she was allowed to eat her dinner at the table with us children. Of course, when she had a tantrum and was spittin' and givin' out abuse, Sister Margaret Mary would drag her off, real quick, to the punishment room, holdin' her fast, and Breege-God-help-her would be bawlin' that she was sorry and she didn't mean it. We used laugh, but still an' all were sorry for her. We might not see her again for maybe a week.

'One day – we couldn't believe our eyes – she thrun the big saucepan with the two grip handles across the kitchen floor and it full of cabbage water. She screamed at Sister Margaret Mary that nuns were nothin' but liars – that some mothers were not dead at all, only too poor to look after their babies. That sometimes girls were not right in the head and so they were taken away from their families. She would be all red in the face and stutherin' like this: "They do get p-p-put away and the nuns come and take the b-b-babies offa them." God tonight, that Breege had a terrible temper.

'Other times, mind you, she could be good, goin' around in a great humour with everyone and sayin' she was sorry for what she done. When she was like that, Sister Margaret Mary would say she was forgiven but she must make a firm resolution to sin no more. Then she would say to us, "Ah poor Breege-God-help-her, there's not much harm in her, but you wouldn't want to pay any heed to what she says."

'So we got used to her ways, but do you know the way it is? Sometimes when I looked at the dent in the side of the big pot, I would remember how it was done, and the sight of it would put the heart across me.'

# Settling In

THUMP THUMP!

At seven thirty every weekday morning, Sister Finbar burst through the spring doors into Blessed Imelda's ward for five to ten-year-old girls. 'In the name of the Father and of the Son and of the Holy Ghost . . .'

'Amen,' children and nurses responded with one voice.

'Oh Jesus, through the most pure heart of Mary, I offer thee all the prayers, works and sufferings, joys and pleasures of this day, for all the intentions of thy Sacred Heart.' Her voice rang out authoritatively and we at once brought the palms of our hands together and closed our eyes, the better to perform our first spiritual task of the day. We could hear her coming long before she appeared through the doors, recognising her sure step along the back corridor, the rustle of her voluminous white habit, the jangle of the huge bunch of keys that hung from her belt. Sister Finbar was the custodian of every cupboard and locker, in charge of every nurse and patient and maker of all decisions concerning the welfare of her ward.

'The Bar is coming . . . the Bar . . . the Bar!' The warning rippled along the ranks of beds. Activity intensified. Out on the veranda, the night nurses tore off the cardigans which they were permitted to wear only through the hours of darkness. Shivering slightly in the early morning frost, they bent over the work which had to be completed before they could go off duty. They washed each one of us from basins filled with tepid water poured from tall enamel jugs, ignoring our protestations as they roused us from our sleep with wet, soapy facecloths. They rubbed our backs with methylated spirit to prevent bedsores, changed wet sheets and fine-combed our heads in readiness for the day.

Sister Finbar intoned the morning prayers in a melodious Cork accent: 'Our Father . . . Hail Mary . . . Glory be to the Father . . . Hail, Holy Queen.' Pacing the ward slowly, she fingered her rosary beads, her florid face unsmiling. Her brilliant blue eyes were never still – probing, seeking out the smallest sign of crisis, epidemic or bad nursing practice. She could spot a septic sore or an infested head before even the sufferer was aware of it. Wherever she found fault, she laid her hand on the steel bedhead as she passed, tapping it lightly with her ringed finger, to indicate that prompt attention was required there as soon as prayers were over.

'These beds are not in a straight line, Nurse – they're a disgrace! There's too much sheet showing here. This child is to have no breakfast as she's for theatre this morning.'

As the pace of activity quickened, Sister Finbar went to the desk in the centre of the ward to read the report of the night's events. Then she unbuttoned her cuffs, rolled up her sleeves and homed in on her chosen tasks, examining a new swelling, adjusting a tight bandage that was causing pain or chafing, cropping and clipping hair that had grown too long to be hygienic.

'If I see a single nit,' she warned, ' the whole lot comes off!'

Small wonder that we prayed so fervently in that first hour of the day. There was so much to cause us anxiety, but almost more than our fear of medical attention, we dreaded the thought of being bald, even though the Bar had given us her word of honour, and we had seen with our own eyes, that a shaven head would soon grow again, thick and curly, so that an ugly little one that you had hardly noticed before became suddenly beautiful as an angel and the envy of us all.

At last, the night nurses melted gratefully away as fresh-faced day staff arrived in twos and threes on the ward. Some wore stern expressions and handled us with great vigour and at top speed to get the worst of their chores over and done with. Others were cheerful and seemed happy in their work. As long as there was no emergency, they sang and chatted to us and to each other. We listened carefully to their talk while they were making our beds, in the hope of hearing the latest gossip.

When the ablutions were over, lumbering breakfast trolleys appeared: porridge in a big steel pot, sometimes thin enough to drink but more often too thick to be parted from the ladle. Bowls piled high with eggs, always hard-boiled: 'Ah, give us a brown one, please, Nurse,' we pleaded. Trays of thick-cut bread scraped with butter. A nurse heaved a huge pot from bed to bed, pouring ready-mixed, milky sweet tea into beakers and the small, spouted pots for those of us lying on our backs.

Later came the bedpans, too late for some, and after that another trolley, set up for the dressing of wounds, with wads of gauze and cotton wool, bottles of iodine, red mercurochrome and gentian violet. Hot, sterile dressings were plucked with long tongs out of a steaming cauldron and waved about in the air until just cool enough to be placed as a hot fomentation over the affected part.

Nearly every patient got a wound or two. These were caused by the bursting of abscesses which formed on the diseased limbs, swelling up the flesh and causing what we called 'crying pain'. That was bad enough, but worse by far was the treatment: the aspirating, which had to be done many times before the abscess was ready to burst open and expel the last of the poison. Aspirations were beyond-crying pain, for all our energy was needed to grip the bed-head as the thick, hollow needle with the syringe attached was plunged into the heart of the swelling, and to call on the help of Jesus and Mary as the poison was drawn out.

Nurse McGinty gave praise when it was over. 'You were very good now,' she would say. 'Isn't that better out than in?'

And when we saw the syringe full of yellow pus, we laughed with pure relief and gave thanks, for the swelling was eased and, with the help of God, there would be no more aspirating for a week, maybe two. In that time, the abscess might ripen and burst of its own accord. So we offered up novenas to our pet saints and watched for spots of blood to appear on soiled dressings, a sure sign that there would soon be an open wound, which was better than an abscess any day.

When the morning tasks were done and we were all looking clean and tidy, the domestic staff appeared with bowls of wet tea leaves, which they scattered across the floor to collect the dust. After sweeping up with broad-headed brooms, they opened tins of sweet-smelling wax and dollopped it around the floor on wooden spoons with the solemnity of priests blessing a crowd with holy water. Finally, they got to work with cloth-covered wooden blocks on long handles and rhythmically polished, swaying back and forth until the floor gleamed, fit for the coming of priest or doctor.

'We are not to be called maids,' they sternly instructed us. 'We are the girls.'

The never-ending torrent of sound was made up of
squeaking trolley wheels, steel instruments scraping on
enamel utensils, the clank and clang of cumbersome
apparatus and children's voices clamouring in high-
pitched competition with the voice of Radio Éireann –
the *Hospitals' Requests* programme was everyone's
favourite. Soon was added the shouting of the school-
teacher – known to us as 'Wastras' – a strange sounding
name which we neither questioned nor realised that it
was 'Máistreás' – the Irish word for school-mistress. With
boundless energy, she battled against the noise and the
nursing priorities, teaching us to read and write with
crayons on small, hand-held blackboards and to say our
prayers, in English and in Irish.

On Sundays, with no school and no doctors' rounds,
there was a bit more peace and quiet on the veranda. Sister Finbar wore a black habit, which somehow softened
her features and made her look smaller. It was an off-duty
kind of look she had, and we found her more approach-
able when she wore it. In the centre of the field facing
the wards, a great, glass-sided altar towered over us. Thirty feet high, it housed a golden tabernacle which could
be seen for miles around. The altar, which had stood in
the middle of O'Connell Bridge during the Eucharistic
Congress of 1932, had been given to the hospital after
that auspicious occasion.

A little to the left of the altar stood a statue of Our
Lady. Through a latticed arch over her head, roses
climbed from the month of May onwards through the
summer, and out of the rockery beneath her feet there
poured white alyssum and tumbling aubrietia. With
devoted application we attempted to draw our Heavenly

Mother in our sketchbooks. Behind my closed eyelids she became mine exclusively, and I put on her the face of my choice. At my bidding she came at once, filling my mind with heavenly light, and was never for an instant distracted from my entreaties.

On Sundays, because a priest came to say mass on the altar in the field, Sister Finbar did not enter through the sprung doors with the morning prayers bursting out of her but appeared suddenly in our midst, taking everyone by surprise. She walked along the veranda at a leisurely pace, stopping here and there for a chat and surveying her domain with pride and good humour. Although not officially at work, she often helped the nurses by distributing from a big basket the assorted woolly hats, which we wore for mass. There was great competition for the best of the hats: they had all been knitted or crocheted by old nuns and simple people, and some of them were such an awful shape you would have a job to keep them on your head at all. There were linen cloths, too, finely embroidered, for the communicants to put under their chins, in case the Host should fall out of the priest's hands before it reached their tongues.

On the six Tuesdays before the Feast of the Assumption, all patients aged six and seven were drawn to a space apart from the rest, to be prepared by Sister Patrick for their first Holy Communion.

Sister Patrick arrived on the first bus from the city. She wore a black habit and carried an attaché case containing catechisms, booklets from the Catholic Truth Society and bundles of holy pictures, held together with elastic bands. These she distributed freely and wrote commemorative messages on the backs of them, in the most perfect handwriting we had ever seen. Her face shone with kindness and good humour, and unlike any other nun we had ever known, she was never impatient or in an urgent hurry, but stayed as long as she could, to talk about Jesus and Mary, until a nurse came to warn her that her bus was waiting for her at the gate. After she had gone, we were left feeling so precious that we could put up with anything that happened or was done to our bodies, and we waited in great excitement for the Feast of the Assumption, which, Sister Patrick assured us, would be the happiest day of our lives.

On Thursdays, Mr Macauley, the orthopaedic surgeon, arrived on the veranda with a group of respectful attendants. The sight of him in his dark suit made some of us fall silent as, with thumping hearts, we watched his slow progress from bed to bed, daring to hope that he was bringing us good news – that we were ready to go home – yet knowing without having to be told that there was no improvement in our condition since his last visit and that some of us were worse than we had been when we first arrived. Home remained as far away as heaven, and so we felt only relief when he gave us a brief nod and passed quickly on to the next bed. It was no joke to become suddenly the subject of a lecture and have students close in around your bed to stare and feel, moving aside gowns and sometimes modesty squares as well.

A silver-haired man of great dignity, Mr Macauley would screw up his face with concentration as he probed deep into a joint with his immaculate white hands, spanning his thumb and little finger across from hip bone to hip bone, working out how much shorter one leg would be than the other when the patient came to walk again. Holding our x-rays up to the light, he pointed out the diseased areas, lecturing to his students in a language that patients could not understand. If an abscess was forming on a limb, Mr Macauley was quick to find it and sometimes marked the spot for the first aspiration by making a cross on the bulging flesh with his fountain pen.

Sister Finbar was always at his elbow, nodding or shaking her head, matching her step to his as they went. Now and then, the great man might catch the eye of the child in the bed and, as though suddenly reminded of the human being, would give a wintry smile or a brief touch on the head.

Later Sister Finbar returned to give us scraps of information. 'Doctor says you're doing grand now, making good progress and the wounds healing nicely, thank God.'

'Will I get off my frame so?'

'Soon, please God.'

'When? How long?'

'Not long,' said the Bar.

And with that we had to be content and only thankful that clinic was over for another week . . . until Nurse McGinty arrived with a trolley to carry out instructions that the Bar had forgotten to mention.

I was not long settling into my new way of life, and as I became familiar with the daily and weekly routines of the hospital, I lost much of my fear. We 'Biddies' lay on our verandas under coverlets of Our Lady's blue, while the 'Johnnies', from whom we were strictly segregated and whom we usually only saw by accident in the treatment areas, had beds covered with red blankets, symbolising the bleeding heart of Jesus. We all also had comfort blankets, which we wrapped around our heads on frosty nights, leaving only the tips of our noses showing. In summer, as the days grew warmer, we lay naked but for our small modesty squares, tanning under the healing rays of the sun.

I came to accept without complaint that I had to be in

hospital, since the stabs of pain still shot through my leg whenever the weight was lifted, and any thought of walking became only a memory. Soon, an abscess began to fester inside my thigh, and from my first experience of aspiration, this became the main source of my worry. If I saw a nurse approaching with a sterile trolley, covered with a cloth to hide the instruments it contained, my heart quickened and I said a quick prayer 'Please don't let it be for me', in the hope that she would pass me by, but I always knew by the painful tightness of my thigh when an aspiration was due.

But the ten days or so between aspirations were peaceful enough, and for much of the time I was kept in good heart by regular visits from Daddy and Paul and the time spent in preparation for my first Holy Communion. I quickly learned to protect myself from the early hostility of some patients by changing my given speech and expressions to the common language of the veranda and by the end of my first month felt myself well integrated into the culture there.

As far as I could see, the only important advantage my fellow patients had over me was their easy familiarity with the Irish language. As I had come without a word of it, I was not favoured by Wastras, who, almost daily, stood unsmiling over my bed, making me repeat the words of the Hail Mary – '*Sé do bheatha a Mhuire, atá lán de ghrásta*' – and after that a litany of useful phrases which I had to learn, parrot fashion.

As long as I was on the weight and pulley, which allowed me to move my upper half, I could still feel some superiority over those who were strapped on to frames from the neck down. But after about six weeks, that solace, too, was removed from me.

'We have to keep you in the right position,' Nurse

McGinty explained in a light-hearted way, as I was wheeled away one afternoon, without warning, to a treatment room on the back corridor. Then the leg which had nothing in the world wrong with it was bound up with gauze bandage to match the bad one. Long strips of sticking plaster were stuck down on either side, with loops at the foot end through which cords were threaded. More bandage over that and, lastly, thin strips of plaster were wound around the leg at regular intervals, to keep it all in place. 'Plenty of gauze now,' Nurse McGinty supervised the work with her arms folded, 'to keep the plaster from cutting into the leg. We can't have any sores that might go septic.'

When all that was done I was lifted up, and the frame with its padded saddle was placed under me. Leather straps were buckled across my body, around my groin and under my knees and ankles. The cords were pulled tightly down below the footplates, anchoring my two legs with complex windings and knots.

I cried at first, feeling it as a punishment, but the nurses kept telling me that it was all done for my own good. 'The position is everything if you're ever going to get better.' Later, Sister Finbar brought me a toy out of St Anthony's storeroom, and sure enough I felt more comfortable than I had for a long time. The firmness of my binding protected me from the jerks and bumps caused by any sudden movement of my bed and I was free of all pain.

'It's only a matter of getting used to it,' they all said.

# A New Patient

I N THE MONTH of June, a new patient arrived by ambulance, and after a day or two of having things done to her inside the ward, her bed was wheeled out to the veranda and put beside mine.

Her name was Eileen Cassidy, and at first sight I was not too happy about having her as a neighbour. I was used to Pauline by now, with her gentle, agreeable ways, on one side and a little one called Una on the other, who was young enough to do as she was told and give me no trouble. Now the new patient was put between us.

Eileen had a loud voice, and there was no trace in her of the shyness of a new girl. Neither did she seem to care that she looked pinched and ugly after having her hair cut off. It was russet red and had fallen down her curved back in thick waves and ringlets before Sister Finbar got at it. The Bar, as always, had done her best to leave a good quiff at the front, using the clippers only on the back of the head, where Eileen could not see the worst of the damage.

When that task was done, Eileen had been put on a spinal frame and now lay bent backwards from the waist, so that her view of the world was upside down. Even her head was held fast by a leather harness strapped around her forehead and chin, with a weight hanging out of it and dangling over the top of her bed. When I asked her how she was getting on, she said the leather stuff made her think of a farmer's horse, but, please God, she would soon get used to it. That gave me a good laugh and I began to like her better.

Sunday came around, and once mass was over, we could look forward to an easy day, free of treatment. As part of the relaxation, the harness was removed from Eileen's head, so she was better able to look around and take in her surroundings. As Sister Finbar approached her bed with the nicest hat she could find in the basket, Eileen squinted up at her curiously.

'Hey, Misther Finbar, come 'ere til I ax 'ou somethin'.'

'What is it, child?'

'Were 'ou ever a girrul?'

'I was.'

'And had 'ou hair on 'ou?'

'I had, of course.'

'An' did another nun cut it off?'

'Yes,' said Sister Finbar, 'it had to be done when I took my final vows as a nun. That's the rule. Now, mine is gone for ever, but yours will grow again, better then before once you're off your frame. If I didn't cut it now, you would get a bald patch on the back of your head and you would be a shocking sight altogether.' She held Eileen's hand in a firm grasp and looked straight into her eyes. Eileen gave her a toothless smile of complete acceptance.

'Now I've put you beside Rosemary,' the Bar went on, 'and there is Pauline on her other side. Won't you all be good to each other now and do everything you are told?'

Eileen told us she had come a long way, from down the country, and although she had eight brothers and sisters, she would have few visitors. Her parents could only come, she said, when there was a special excursion bus, and even then they might not always have the handy money for the fare.

'My daddy comes every Sunday,' I told her, 'and my brother on Wednesdays, on his half-day off school. I do get loads of presents, and I'll be making my first Holy Communion in August, on the Feast of the Assumption.'

She looked at me in a cheeky way that made me think I might have met my match.

'So will I,' she said. ''Ou're not the only one.'

Some time later I asked her, 'Do you like sago?'

'I do,' said Eileen. 'Sure, I'd eat anything.'

'If you eat my sago, I'll let you play with Marjorie.'

I held up my beautiful doll, who I kept all day by my side. Some other children had dolls but there were none to compare with Marjorie, who was two feet tall, with real hair and eyes that opened and closed. When tipped forward, a sound like 'Mama' issued from an opening in her back and her arms and legs were jointed. She wore a pink silk dress, long-legged bloomers trimmed with lace, real leather shoes and white socks.

'My daddy bought her in Singer's, the sewing machine shop on Grafton Street,' I told Eileen. 'There's not anther doll like her in the whole world.'

'Imagine that!' Now her face was full of awe, as if she was seeing a holy apparition.

'Oh, yes. She was a mannequin in the window, showing off her gorgeous clothes.'

'I'll eat 'our sago, all right,' Eileen promised, clearly wondering what, in God's name, a mannequin could be, 'and 'our porridge, too. Anything 'ou don't like, I'll eat.'

'Right you are then.' I stretched out my hand and Eileen grasped it eagerly. 'Pull!' I commanded. With a couple of jerks, we managed to turn the castors of our beds sideways, the two beds came together with a clang, and I placed my treasure in Eileen's arms. Holding her reverently, Eileen examined the doll all over, stroked her hair and peered up her skirt.

''Ou could have that for an abscess,' she suggested with her finger on the soundbox, 'and put a dressing on it.'

'Gimme back that doll.' I snatched Marjorie out of Eileen's hands and hugged her close, as though having arrived in the nick of time, to rescue her from mortal danger. 'Marjorie is not a patient,' I shouted. 'Marjorie is perfect in every way.'

# THE BEST VISITOR

IT WAS ALWAYS Daddy who got off the bus on Sunday afternoons. Every week I looked past him as he came through the gates, just in case there was someone with him, but except for the odd time when he brought a friend or a neighbour from Sandycove to visit me, he was always alone. We watched for him, Pauline, Eileen and myself, and others too, who soon learned how much fun his visits were. From our first, distant glimpse of him, we were beckoning with our hands and shouting for him to hurry on over and let us see what he had brought for us.

Everyone on the veranda enjoyed my daddy's visits. He came every Sunday without fail, bringing the *Dandy*, the *Beano* and *Playbox* comics and two bulging bags of Lemon's Pure Sweets for sharing out. He sang us songs with ridiculous words and told jokes that had us in stitches. When the Bar was out of sight, he had a laugh with the nurses and gave them cigarettes, which they hid in their pockets to enjoy when they went off duty.

Sister Finbar's face was pink and smiling whenever she came to talk to Daddy, and she blessed him for his gift of making merry. 'Aren't you great,' she would say, 'the way you cheer us all up?'

The first thing he did on arrival was to empty his pockets of the surprises, then he set about entertaining us with made-up news from Sandycove.

'Father Barrett fell out of the pulpit yesterday.'

'Get away with you.'

'Yes, he did. Do you know why?'

'No, tell us!'

'Because the Canon went BOODOOM!'

Daddy so enjoyed Eileen's hearty giggle and her gummy grin that he poked her in the arm and said, 'Listen, I'll tell you again,' and Eileen obliged him every time by shrieking with laughter, even at the third and fourth telling.

Then he sang: 'Oh, I must go and see my mudder – because I want some bread and budder – All the way to Poolaphuca – Nithery-nootin, nithery-nootin.'

'Sure that's not a word at all,' we challenged him, sometimes disdainfully, if we thought he was getting too stupid.

'It's a very good word indeed,' Daddy insisted, 'nithery-nootin.'

'What does it mean then?'

'Well, it means . . . ah well, it doesn't matter what it means. It sounds nice and makes the song more interesting.' Then he sang it again, lifting the legs of his trousers and dancing up and down between the beds, pretending to trip over his feet.

'Hasn't he lovely, shiny shoes on him?' Pauline said admiringly. She was always interested in what the visitors had on their feet.

Sometimes I got a letter from Mummy, saying how much she missed me, but she had visited me only twice since I came to Cappagh, and it was many weeks now since I had seen her.

'She's not very well, darling,' Daddy explained, 'but she will come when the weather gets better.'

I remembered how poor Mummy had cried, the day

she brought me here; how Sister Finbar had led her away quickly so I would not see. But I did see and, in a way, was pleased to see her so upset by my illness. All the same, I did not want her to be ill and maybe die of a broken heart, so I prayed every day for her speedy recovery and wrote letters to cheer her up, telling her that really I was doing very well and my abscess was clearing up nicely.

Much as I longed to be at home, I soon stopped asking the question, 'How long will I be here?' for the only answer I could get from the Bar was, 'Not long, with the help of God'. For the same reason, I had stopped asking when I would see my mother again, for there was no good answer to that one either.

Once I heard Daddy telling the Bar in a low voice, 'She finds it so upsetting . . .' She answering, 'I know, I know,' clutching his arm and shaking her head in the urgent way adults do when something is said that children are not supposed to hear.

In one of her letters, Mummy wrote: *I think of you every single evening at seven o'clock, so you must think of me, too, and in that way, we will always be in touch. It will be our little secret. Don't forget now, seven o'clock on the dot!* The letter was signed: *Mummy, with so much love.*

Every evening after the prayers, I closed my eyes again and thought about Mummy. I saw her in a pool of light, wearing some kind of floating garment and with no make-up on her face. Holding her arms out to me, she repeated every time the solemn promise: 'I will come soon, my beloved child, if you are very good and do everything that you are told.'

# TING-A-LING, TING-A-LING

THE FIFTEENTH OF August arrived at last – the day on which the mother of God was taken up to heaven, body and soul, without having to get sick and die. A great feast, Sister Patrick taught us, which we were privileged to celebrate in the best possible way, by receiving her beloved son into our hearts for the first time.

In a cleared space on the veranda, we first communicants lay side by side, outstanding in our beauty and our saintliness. If we were to die today, we, too, would be taken straight to heaven. Almost afraid to move, for fear of disturbing our adornment, we waited as patiently as we could for the priest to arrive.

The final preparations had begun two days ago, when we made our first confessions to the Finglas priest, bravely whispering our sins of thought, word, deed and omission into his large, purple ear.

On the great day itself, our bodily preparation began as soon as the day nurses came on duty. After being subjected to vigorous washing and brushing, we were dressed in beautiful white gowns and veils, which were anchored somehow to our heads by wreaths of waxen flowers and spread out over our pillows. Our bedheads, too, were draped with veiling, with small posies of flowers pinned here and there, so that each bed looked like a little shrine, with ourselves in the middle like holy statues. Near by, a small table covered with a starched, linen cloth was set with a finger bowl, a silver paten and a vase of fresh flowers, where the priest would on this occasion perform his ablutions especially for us.

Nurses and girls came by to admire us, some with tears in their eyes. 'Say a prayer for us, won't you?' they begged.

'I will,' Eileen promised, 'if I don't die of the hunger first.'

'Wouldn't you think,' Nurse McGinty said, 'that on this occasion, at least, you would make an effort to behave yourself! The fasting will do you no harm and – only if you're good – you will get a special breakfast of rashers and eggs as soon as mass is over.'

At the appointed hour, a small nun came running out from the angle of the wards, ringing a silver bell. *Ting-a-ling, ting-a-ling*, the sound commanded us, *'The blessed sacrament approaches . . . Bow down, bow down' . . . Ting-a-ling, ting-a-ling.*

Behind her strode the magnificent, vested figure of Father Feckler, a visiting German Jesuit, a huge man. The little nun was barely half his size. He had a long, flowing beard, and he bore in his hands a chalice brimming with wafers, which would soon be made sacred. Preceded by his server, he crossed the field and mounted the steps of the altar to begin the mass.

Silence descended over the Johnnies and the Biddies as all watched and waited for the weekly miracle to take place inside the glass chapel. Nuns and nurses stopped in their tracks and knelt on the cold floor of the veranda. We, who were well prepared for this great day, recited the now familiar prayers, begging to be made worthy of the sacrament. Reading from our first missals with the pearly white covers, we followed with our fingers the translated words of the mass.

Those patients who were not among the privileged gaped at us in awe and respect. They had been told to offer prayers for us today, just as we, in return, must pray for them. Little ones, who had not reached the use of reason, stared around them in wonder at the strangeness of the silence, which in a little while was broken by the ringing of the sanctus bell, rung by the serving nun with all her might, so that the sound carried across the field to the road and as far as the village itself. The sound startled the crows nesting in the tall trees behind the altar. As the priest raised the host above his head, they flew out in disarray, swooping over the silent ranks of beds.

> *Caw caw, ting-a-ling . . . 'Blessed is he who comes in the name of the Lord' . . . Caw caw, ting-a-ling.*

The disturbance caused Eileen to break out in a fit of giggles. Sister Finbar's head jerked up from her prayers to see who was misbehaving. Pauline and I pressed our hands tightly over our faces in a desperate effort not to laugh. I breathed the emergency prayer which never failed me in moments of temptation. 'Jesus, mercy! Mary, help!'

'He is coming,' the Bar murmured, just loud enough for us to hear. 'He will soon be in our hearts.'

The priest swept down on to the veranda. The serving nun picked up the paten from the side table and held it in turn under our chins as, bending low over our beds, the priest tenderly placed a host on each of our tongues. I lay with my eyes tightly closed and felt the sanctifying grace coursing through my body as he declared in a strong voice, *'Corpus Domini nostri Jesu Christi, custodiat animam tuam in vitam aeternam.'*

Silently I responded, 'Oh Lord, I am not worthy that thou shouldst enter under my roof, but only say the word and my soul shall be healed.'

'You children,' Father Feckler boomed, coming down from the convent after his breakfast, 'vil haf a high place in heaven. You vil be held in the arms of Jesus and Mary, mit garlands of golden roses in your hair. Your purgatory vil be very short – perhaps no purgatory at all for you – for you are God's special little children, chosen to suffer mit Him. God bless and keep you all.'

He showed his great white teeth in a smile that testified to this wonderful news, and he blew up balloons and tied them to our bedheads. He gave us holy pictures and asked us to pray for him and also for little black children who do not know God. 'The prayers of children', he assured us, 'are the most powerful force on earth. Today, Our Blessed Lord vil refuse you nothing.'

We felt shy in his presence and lost for words, for we had never in our lives seen such a long beard, except on holy pictures. But after he had gone, as we tucked into our own breakfast, we feasted our minds on the vision he had revealed to us and were especially thrilled about the golden roses. 'Well, I only hope,' said Eileen, whose veil was by now all askew, 'that we will have a decent bit of hair on us by then, or we'll look as daft as Kathleen O'Donnell does in that baggy oul' hat.'

# NIGHT LIFE

SISTER JOAN LOOKED far too old to be still a nurse and was, in every way but dress, more like a nun. She had been in Cappagh since the hospital first opened in 1908 and knew everything there was to know about every patient, even though some of the children had never set eyes on her.

Sister Joan was in charge of the whole hospital during the hours of darkness. She was never seen on the wards during the day, but any patient who happened to be awake just before midnight would see her moving along the ranks of beds on her heavy legs, wearing a dark cloak over her uniform and a starched veil pulled low on her forehead, with not a bit of hair showing. She was always punctual, and the night nurses were kept on their toes, watching for the beam of her torch, for if they were foolish enough to be caught with their arms folded or their feet propped up on the desk, Sister Joan would soon have them scattered in all directions, only too ready to point out chores that were left undone. She would stand over them, giving out instructions in a rasping whisper: 'Which child has the temperature? Did she get her tablets? What time was that exactly? You didn't leave her outside, did you? Get her into the ward this minute.'

No child who had ever suffered a spell of sickness of the fevered kind and was marked down for special watching

during the night would ever in her life forget the experience of lifting her heavy eyelids to see the stiff white veil
hovering over her, like the wings of a ghostly bird, and feel
the rapid breath of the night sister on her hot face. 'Good
child! Go back to sleep now. You'll be grand in the morning, please God.'

'Do you know Sister Joan?' I asked two nurses as they
were making my bed one morning in the early days.

'No,' said one, who had not been long in Cappagh,
'who is she?'

'Oh, I know,' said the other, 'you mean Night Sister
Joan. I've never seen her myself, but I've heard enough
about her. She's the scourge of the night nurses, the way
she tries to catch them out, and she leaves reports for the
Bar, complaining about everyone and everything.'

'She's very experienced, I suppose,' said the first nurse.

'Experienced, is it! She's out of the Ark!'

'She does wake me up and spoil my sleep,' I said.

The nurses laughed. 'Well, she has to do that, to make
sure you're still alive!'

Some would say that Sister Joan was not a real person
at all but the apparition of a dead nurse, who came back
to haunt the veranda and keep the children safe. Yet she
was nothing like a saint or an angel to our minds, but
more on the lines of the leprechauns and lost souls, of
which we were all at first afraid, and which some would
swear they had seen for themselves, wafting in from the
fields and floating over our beds in the blackest part of
the night.

Sister Joan seemed real enough to me, for she made
too much noise for a ghost. But I could not get rid of the
deep-down fear that if I said I did not believe in all the
superstitious stories that were told and ghosts really did
exist after all, I might suffer a terrible fate at their hands,

as soon as Sister Joan's back was turned. We three spoke bravely enough to each other, pretending that nothing could scare us as long as we said our prayers, especially those Acts of Perfect Contrition, whispered hotly into our blankets, last thing before we slept. At least then, if the worst happened, our souls would be saved and the golden roses would be our everlasting reward.

'Oh my God, I am heartily sorry for having offended Thee, and I detest my sins above every other evil because they displease Thee, my God, Who for Thine infinite goodness art so deserving of all my love, and I firmly resolve by Thy holy grace never more to offend Thee and to amend my life, amen.'

If little Una O'Malley had the misfortune to be awake for the coming of Sister Joan, despite all assurances of her good intentions, Una would tell us that her heart banged like a drum inside her chest. She was afraid that one of those times she would be smothered by her comfort blanket, which she pressed tightly over her nose and mouth for fear of uttering a sound that would draw attention to herself.

Una's bed was next to Pauline's, on the junior side of ours, and for much of the time she watched our carry-on with a kind of longing and admiration for our bravado. Sometimes we included her in our activities or gave her some little thing, because Sister Finbar said we were to be good to her, but she was, in our eyes, only a young one who was not much use in a game. On the other hand, because she believed everything we told her, we got some fun out of telling her tall stories, which often had her crying out in terror.

'Watch out for the little white hand,' I warned her in a solemn voice. 'It moves along the back corridor, knocking on every pane of glass. I saw it one time, when I was in at the back of the ward, a little baby's hand bunched into a fist, knock-knock-knocking and a small voice crying, "Save me! Save me!" It would break your heart to hear it.'

Una's face turned the colour of porridge, so I pressed on, 'One night, a nurse went out to see what was going on. The passage was full of blue smoke, the crying grew louder and louder, and the nurse fell down in a dead faint.'

'Stop! Stop!' Una pressed her hands over her ears and shut her eyes. 'Please don't tell me any more!'

'All right then, I won't upset you.' I pretended sympathy but all I did was bide my time until she was off her guard, then I finished the story in a rush. 'That nurse went queer in the head. She went into an enclosed order and spent the rest of her life offering up prayers for the souls in limbo.'

'Now, you've told a lie!' Eileen had stayed quiet only long enough to catch me out. 'Sure where's the good in praying for unbaptised babies, that can never get into heaven anyway.'

'Shut your gob,' I said. 'I hate you!'

'Shh! Ah, now, will yez give over. Pauline tried to intervene but Eileen shouted her down.

'Listen to me, Una, I've a better one. Didn't I find this little small pair of shoes on my pillow one morning. They were a present from the leprechauns, to thank me for leavin' a saucer of milk under the bed for them. All night long I could hear the sound of hammer-hammer-hammer, little silver tinkles comin' out of my locker, and in the mornin', when the nurses went to get out my wash bag, there was this little small pair of green leather shoes. The nurses couldn't see 'em, of course, only myself. Gorgeous they were, that's God's truth. The leprechauns will bring 'ou luck, if 'ou leave milk out for 'em.'

'Sure how could I? I haven's a saucer and I can't reach the floor,' cried Una frantically.

'Isn't it queer, all the same,' I said, 'the way no one saw them shoes but yourself?'

'They were lost,' Eileen insisted. 'They must have fell on the floor and got swep' up by the girls.'

'Now who's telling lies? You'll have to tell that one in confession.'

Eileen leaned far out and yanked my bed over with a crash that nearly jerked me on to the floor. 'I'll give 'ou a little white fist,' she yelled, and her face was as red as her hair as she punched me about the head. She was far too quick for me to get a swipe at her and was back lying dead straight on her frame, looking as though butter wouldn't melt in her mouth, by the time a nurse arrived to see what all the shouting was about.

'She hit me.'

The nurse pulled our beds apart and set us back squarely on our mattresses. 'The two of you will get a wallop that you won't forget if Nurse McGinty hears you.'

Una watched the scene with enormous, tear-filled eyes. What kind of a place was this that she had come into? Who would give her comfort? She was so far away from home and all that she loved. There was only that Auntie – well, she said she was an Auntie, that woman who came sometimes on a Sunday with a bottle of red lemonade. She sat there talking without taking a breath for the whole of the visiting hour. Una had never seen or heard of her before coming to Cappagh, but she couldn't accuse her of telling lies when she said she was a cousin of her dad's, only too pleased to visit as she only lived in Glasnevin. 'The dead centre of Dublin. Ha! Ha! Isn't that a good one?' Una was always polite and laughed when a laugh seemed to be expected. The lemonade came in handy, of course, for sharing with us in exchange for a bit of attention, but she was always glad when the visits were over, for she could never think of anything to say.

How could you tell a stranger about all the things that haunted you? The terrible fears that the nurses said were silly and even Wastras, who knew the answer to everything, said were only in your imagination and could, like everything else, be overcome by prayer and good behaviour.

It was Pauline who one day provided the best hope of consolation. Seeing that Una was upset and crying into the crook of her arm, she asked a nurse to pull their beds together, just for a few minutes. The nurse was happy to oblige, and Pauline spoke gently into Una's ear. 'Don't be cryin' now, they do be always fightin' but there's no harm in them.' As she spoke, she removed from her neck a square of brown felt, sewn on to a fine cord. With some difficulty she lowered it over Una's head. 'Take this scapular,' she said. 'It has a piece of a saint's bone in it. Keep it on you at all times and no evil can get to you.'

Una received the gift with tears running down her cheeks and kept it clutched in her hand all day. But that night, as on all others, she was again visited in her sleep by weird, floating shapes and, in the small hours of the morning, was jerked into wakefulness by the sound that she dreaded more than anything else in the world: the keening and moaning of the Banshee, approaching across the field in a rush of wind, to visit some unfortunate child whose name had a 'Mac' or an 'O' in front of it. On finding that child, we had told her, the hideous crone would stand over the bed, combing her streely hair and moaning, moaning without rest, bringing news of a death in the family.

# KATHLEEN

THE HUMP ON Kathleen O'Donnell's back was so big that she was not able to lie flat on her bed at all. We were told to treat her kindly because she was delicate. That was why she had to stay inside the ward all the time and only came out to the veranda when the weather was warm. She did not have much in the way of company in there, except when another patient was brought inside for some unusual reason and put beside her for a short while, or when one of the girls, stealing a short break, leaned on her broom for a rest and a chat.

Kathleen had a couple of small dolls in the bed with her but was not often seen playing with them, and she never complained about her isolation from the veranda. 'Ah no, sure I wouldn't be able,' she would say, shaking her head, if any kind of effort was asked of her. She was always cheerful and seemed to get enjoyment enough out of being a special case and by airing her views to anyone who would listen.

She squatted frog-like on her bed, hung about with medals and scapulars, and took in everything that happened in the world of Blessed Imelda's ward, whether she was meant to or not. Her small, darting eyes instantly picked up signs of unusual movement or cause for alarm, while others played on, unheeding. She could give advance warning of an enema or an aspiration by the actions of the nurses, the sudden appearance of a trolley or a screen, sure signs that something horrible was going to be done to someone.

'Who is that for, Nurse?' she would ask. 'Who is gettin' that enema?'

'Mind your own little business now.' She was often told off, but having no business of her own to mind, she persisted with her enquiries and never took offence.

'Is it for Rosemary? Is she havin' an op?' Her voice had a note of hope in it. 'Ah, go on, tell me who it's for! I won't say anything, swear to God, I won't.'

As soon as an unfortunate patient, pale with shock and anxiety, was pulled inside, Kathleen was ready with her counsel. 'Offer it up now, whatever they're goin' to do to ya, and I'll be sayin' a prayer for ya.'

Kathleen got on our nerves. We called her names and shouted at her to drop dead. She didn't care. There was usually some grown-up around to take her part and accuse us of being cruel and uncharitable. But if, as sometimes happened, a nurse was annoyed with her, Kathleen had her trump card – a gift that God had given her, we supposed, to make up for the hump. It was a voice of almost unbearable sweetness, a small, pure sound that could cool tempers and nearly persuade you to forgive her for being so nosy and for enjoying the misfortunes of others.

When Kathleen started singing, the nurses would go all soft and, pausing in their work, would say, 'Hush! Be quiet for a minute, can't you, and listen to Kathleen!' Then Kathleen, knowing her power, would summon up all her strength and sing:

*If I were a blackbird I'd whistle and sing,*
*And I'd follow the ship that my true love sails in.*
*Beyond the top mizzen I'd there build my nest*
*And I'd billow my head on his lily-white breast.*

Then the nurses made a great fuss of Kathleen, picked things up for her and brought her beakers of warm, creamy milk. Her face would lift into an elfin smile. Whenever she felt neglected, her silver tinkle of a voice could be heard, going on and on, for you could not stop her once she got started – song after song, every verse word perfect and never a one left out. Only when the charmed nurses moved away did we scream at her, 'Will ya shut yer gob, Kathleen, and give us a bit of peace!'

Every Sunday, the minute mass was over, Kathleen called out to the veranda, 'Is yer daddy comin' today, Rosemary?' I would pretend not to hear her for she knew right well that he would be there, that he never missed going in for a chat with her, never left without giving her something and praising her beautiful voice. For Kathleen, my daddy was better than a visitor of her own. On the few occasions when her own mother had come up from the country, she had brought nothing from the shops but only a round of soda bread with a cross cut into the top of it that she would have baked herself before leaving home that morning. If the nurses saw it, they would take it away to cut up and spread with butter for the tea, but more often, if Kathleen could keep it hidden, the bread would get stuffed into her locker and lie there for a week. When found, it would have gone green and have to be thrown out.

'I hope yer da brings the Galtee cheese,' she would persist, and I would get no rest until I gave her some kind of an answer like, 'He might, but you won't be getting any of it.' But Kathleen only laughed, for she knew that wasn't the way it would be.

In the afternoon, as the visitors began to arrive, the singing would start again.

> *If you ever go across the sea to Ireland,*
> *Be it only at the closing of your days . . .*

# CHRISTMAS

ON CHRISTMAS DAY the hospital was closed to visitors. There were no buses to bring them, even if they had been allowed to come, but none of us minded. We were too excited by the activity going on around us and the prospect of a visit from Santa Claus.

The wards were decorated with blue and yellow garlands of twisted crepe paper and branches of holly from the surrounding hedgerows. The nurses had sprigs of tinsel stuck in their veils, and since all but their essential duties were suspended for the day, they threw themselves wholeheartedly into the spirit of the feast. They laughed and joked with us as they served up the rashers and eggs – a special-occasion treat – and piled up trolleys with toys and games that had been arriving at the hospital for weeks past. The parcels came from kindly people and charities all over Ireland. A good number of them were mine by rights, brought in by Daddy from relations and friends in Sandycove, but as usual Sister Finbar decided, without my permission, that I should keep only a few of them. So I chose a shiny black box of paints and two books, sent by my godmother who was a librarian in London. The rest were put on the trolley for those in need. After breakfast Sister Finbar did the rounds with an open tin of sweets.

'Here comes Santy!' The announcement was made halfway through the morning, and as soon as the figure

57

in red appeared, we burst into cheers and clapping, even though we knew it was only Mr Kenefick dressed up.

Mr Kenefick was the only other person who had been in Cappagh for as long as Sister Joan. Once he had been a handyman, but he was so old now that the only job he was able for was to dress up as Santy on Christmas Day and give out the presents. For years, we were told, he had thrown himself into the part and looked great because he had a real, long beard, but 'Ah, the poor soul,' the nurses said, remarking that he wasn't quite so nimble on his feet these days.

In spite of this warning and appeal to our better natures to make allowances for an old man, our first sight of Mr Kenefick came as a shock. There was nothing jolly about about him at all. His red cloak looked too big for him and the eyes peering out from the red hood were all watery, as if he was barely able to hold back his tears. You couldn't imagine him having a laugh or saying 'Ho! Ho! Ho!' with his hands on his hips.

Eileen and I agreed that not even the smallest and most stupid patients would be fooled by his disguise, and even if they were, they would only be horrified to think of the real Santy being in such poor condition, with his beard all rusty and only one or two loose old teeth in the black hole that was his mouth.

We could see that Sister Finbar and all the nurses were fond of the old man. They helped him on his way with steadying hands and words of encouragement, as if he was a child patient, learning to walk.

'Did yez all write a lether to Santy?' Mr Kenefick asked everyone the same question. 'What did yez ax for?' As he did his round of the veranda, two nurses pushed the trolley in his wake, serving up the presents and telling him the name of each child.

'Would 'ou have such a thing as a dolls' hospital?' Eileen asked when her turn came.

'I would not,' said Mr Kenefick crossly. 'That's not a correct kind of thing to be axin' for. What else do ye want?'

'What about a magic wand then?'

Mr Kenefick looked confused and turned to the nurse. 'What'll we do with her at all?'

'They're not giving out wands this year,' the nurse replied, quick as a flash, 'and you have to be specially trained, or God knows what mischief you'd be up to.' She led him away to the next bed as fast as she could, to save the poor man from any more of Eileen's chat.

'Any little thing at all,' Pauline said when asked what she wished for. For giving no trouble, she was rewarded, as I so often noticed she was, with an extra parcel.

I accepted my parcel with due thanks, though it contained nothing more than a colouring book and a box of crayons.

When Mr Kenefick came to Una O'Malley's bed, she was clutching her rosary beads under the bedclothes and her lips moved in silent prayer, for this old man was no more welcome at her bedside than a Banshee or a leprechaun, even if he was to bring her a crock of gold itself. As he bent over to ask her a question, she lay rigid and staring and could not bring herself to answer his questions or even take her present from his unsteady hands. Mr Kenefick did not seem to notice anything amiss, but told her she was a good girl and left her parcel balanced on her chest.

'Of course, a dolls' hospital is not a Christmassy kind of a present,' Eileen decided, after she discovered that her parcel contained enough consolation to ease her disappointment. 'I'll grant 'ou that. But I'll start a novena tonight to Saint Jude, the patron saint of hopeless cases. That way, I might get a dolls' hospital for my birthday.'

# FEVER

IN THE NEW Year, one of the Johnnies caught diphtheria and had to be sent to the fever hospital. All eyes turned in fear and fascination towards the ambulance as it drove through the gates and stopped in front of Saint Joseph's veranda. Two men in long green overalls jumped out and disappeared into the back of the ward, re-emerging only moments later with the still figure, wrapped in his red blanket and strapped on to a stretcher. The Johnny was shot quickly into the ambulance, the doors were slammed and it took off again at speed, leaving us all to wonder what terrible goings-on lay in store for the poor lad at the end of his journey.

Fearsome stories were told about the fever hospital. It was said that once you went in the doors no one was allowed to visit you, so no one could tell what terrible things might be done to you. You were given a number, and the only way your family could find out how you were getting on was to look in the *Evening Herald*, where a list appeared on the back page, alongside the sports results. All the numbers were there, under three headings:

**Doing Well**
**Progress Satisfactory**
**Not So Well**

If your number was in the first or second group, that was good news, but if you were in the third group, it

61

meant that you were dying, maybe already dead by the time the newspaper arrived on the streets.

'I hope you get sent to the fever hospital!' was a curse we sometimes used when we fell out with each other. But that was before we saw with our own eyes one of our number being whisked away from the world, maybe never to be seen again. We were used to the sight of ambulances coming and going. Some were very clean and comfortable, with the attendants dressed in smart uniforms. But the ambulance that took our Johnny away was old and shabby and seemed to us to add to the shame of the place it had come from. At the sight of it, we made the sign of the cross and feared for ourselves, for we knew that it was only too easy to catch one of many contagious diseases: diptheria, scarletina or even smallpox, that would leave your face pock-marked for the rest of your life, if you were lucky enough to survive the fever. We had also heard a rumour that the fever hospital was so overcrowded that there were two patients to every bed.

'Absolute rubbish,' Nurse McGinty said, and forbade us even to think such a thing. 'We must be grateful that such places exist to give the proper kind of nursing and stop the diseases from spreading. I can assure you that the patients in that hospital are treated as well as in any other. They just have to be kept in isolation until they get better.'

'Or die!' was our unspoken response to that. One of the big Biddies had a brother who had died not long since in the fever hospital, and the word travelled down the veranda that she knew the truth of it. The story went that her mother had had to pretend to be a charwoman, wearing an overall and carrying a bucket with her, the way she could get into the hospital to see her son, and he gasping his last. She it was who had seen them all, two to a bed.

'There's nothing wrong in that,' Pauline said, with some surprise. 'We sometimes had to share beds in the orphanage, if a crowd came in.'

'Well, that's all very well,' I said, 'as long as you're not dying.'

We were all in agreement, though, that dying or not, our Johnny would be sure to have a bed to himself, because of the awkwardness of his spinal frame.

Sister Finbar ordered us not to be worried about catching the disease but to pray our hardest that it would not spread any further and offer up our Holy Communion for the speedy recovery of the unfortunate boy. Precautions had to be taken, of course, so we would all be given injections, and no visitors would be allowed into Cappagh for the next six weeks.

We accepted the bad news and our sore arms without protest. Rules were rules, and after all, wasn't it better to be in Cappagh without visitors than to be dying in the fever hospital and maybe having to share our beds with strangers?

Sunday came, and when the visitors arrived on the bus, they found the gates closed against them and members of staff waiting to explain the situation. All they could do was to stand along the boundary hedges and wave to us across the field. We spotted my daddy at once. He had found something to stand on and remained long after others got fed up and fell away, a comical figure who seemed to be dancing along the top of the hedge, waving his arms and his hat.

'Would ya look at the cut of him?' We laughed and yelled at the tops of our voices. 'Did ya bring the Lemon's Pure Sweets, Misther?

'Have 'ou the Galtee cheese?'

The sweets and presents arrived later, with names

scribbled on paper bags. Sister Finbar, as usual, distributed everything in proper portion, peering into the bags
and dipping her fingers – taking from one to give to
another.

The period of isolation passed very slowly but it had
its compensations. Some children were delighted to
receive the first letters of their lives, and almost every day
there were parcels in the post for someone. I got my
sweets and comics tightly packed in a cardboard carton
and always a letter, too ridiculous for words, written in
Daddy's big, untidy handwriting. Mummy wrote letters,
too, saying how badly she was missing me and promising
that she would try her best to visit me as soon as we were
out of quarantine.

As I read her letters over and over and sucked my
sweets small, my heart would be full to bursting point
with love for my mummy. I saw her lovely face in every
bright light and in the shapes of clouds, and every night
I told her all my secrets, at seven o'clock on the dot.

On the days that should have brought the visitors, the
Finglas bus arrived empty at the gates. 'There it is,' we
remarked without excitement. We listened to the running engine until it changed its tone, then we knew it was
turning in the road, to make its useless way back to the
city.

But no one else caught the diphtheria, and not long
after the gates were opened to the visitors once more, the
afflicted Johnny was returned to his rightful place on
Saint Joseph's veranda, to the cheers and whistles of
Johnnies and Biddies alike.

# Pauline on Her Feet

THE FIRST DUTY of an up-patient was to pick things up from the floor. If we asked the nurses they would usually say, 'Tch, tch! don't be annoying us when we have so much to do. Ask the girls.' The girls, who were always quick to take offence, might well set their faces into hard lines and sweep away our fallen sweets, ribbons, even holy pictures, just to show the nurses that they also had more than enough to do without bending over all the time and maybe doing damage to their backs.

When the worst of the winter was over, Pauline became, unexpectedly, an up-patient. Not a very useful one, but on her feet for an hour in the afternoons and so expected to do her share of the picking up. It took two nurses ten minutes to get Pauline into her splints and lace up her boots in readiness for her golden hour. When lying in her bed, she was completely useless and hadn't the power in her hands to pull two beds together. Pauline looked skinnier and whiter than ever, and when she closed her eyes, the lids were veined with blue. When I reached out to Pauline to pull her bed over for a game, her hand felt like a bird's claw, and it was easy to imagine that if I was to squeeze too hard, her bones would crumble like biscuits in my hand.

I took great pride in my own strong arms and firm,

brown skin. Whoever I decided to play with, Pauline or Eileen or indeed both of them together, it was mainly my strength that dislodged the castors of their beds and brought them to safe berth beside my own.

Eileen, too, was nimble enough and soon became expert at slipping out of her straps to lean out dangerously from her bed, carry out the task of the moment with remarkable speed, then wriggle back into position on her spinal frame before the nurses were any the wiser. Even when suspected of some boldness, as was often the case, she could put on an innocent look and her comical grin seldom failed to bring out the best in those who had intended to punish her.

I found it very hard to accept that Pauline had become an up-patient before me, even if she had, as Eileen pointed out, been in Cappagh for more than a year and a half while we had been there for not quite a year.

'Anyway, she's an orphan,' Eileen added, as if that made Pauline all the more deserving of an answer to her prayers.

When I first heard of Pauline's good fortune, I cried into my blanket with mad jealousy until my throat ached and the blood boiled in my cheeks. By the afternoon I had a high temperature and was pulled in from the veranda to lie in misery and loneliness at the back of the ward.

'Aha,' said the Bar, sticking something that looked like a shoehorn down my throat. 'The tonsils are up. We'll keep you inside tonight, for observation.'

'What's observation?' I asked, fearing some unknown kind of treatment.

'It means keeping an eye on you,' she laughed. The decision made me feel worse than ever.

Once harnessed and upright on the floor, Pauline glowed with pride and determination as she propelled herself up and down the veranda, her claw-hands clutching at the air as she forced one callipered leg in front of the other. In the early days, a nurse walked beside her to keep her steady, but after a week or so, she was left to fend for herself. 'Just give us a shout if you get stuck,' the nurse told her. 'We won't be far away.'

'Pick up that doll's sock, Pauline.'

'Can you get that pencil? I think it rolled under the bed.'

'. . . my sweet . . . my book . . .'

Pauline was always happy to oblige if she could, for she had never been so popular. But the picking-up process was so slow that we rolled our eyes up into our heads with the exasperation of waiting. At the speed of a snail, she lowered herself down the leg of the bed, her lips moving in silent prayer, for fear of falling over and being unable to get up again with all the weight of metal and strapping around her body. On reaching the floor she would clutch at the dropped treasure and tuck it under the bar of her calliper. Then, as she began her ascent, we would offer our hands for her to cling to until she could get a hold on the solidness of the bedhead. As soon as she was back on her feet again, she laughed with relief and started showing off.

'Amn't I great, all the same? Didn't I do very well?'

We would agree that she was improving all the time, and I, having recovered from my jealousy, sometimes allowed her extra playing time with Marjorie to reward her for her trouble – that is, if Pauline was able to stay awake long enough. By the time she was safely back in her bed, she hardly had the strength to eat her tea.

Other days did not end so well. Once, when she was

far down the veranda, Pauline became dizzy and lost her nerve. Clinging to the nearest bedhead, she sobbed and pleaded in her small voice to be rescued.

'Nu . . . urse,' a chorus of voices went up, 'Pauline's in a bad way!'

'I'll be there in a jiffy,' a nurse called back in the same, sing-song tones.

'Tell her to hurry. Say I'm crying.'

'Nu . . . urse, Pauline says she's crying.'

At last the nurse arrived and, laughing, swept Pauline up into her arms. 'Good girl yourself, Pauline. You'll be running races before we know it, and then we'll have to chase you to get you back to bed!'

As her straps were undone and the boots eased off her feet, Pauline shook her head from side to side, crying, 'I'll stay safe in my bed from now on. I don't care if I never walk again.' Completely spent, she was unable even to shove her arm up the sleeve of her bedgown.

In the quiet of the evening, when the night nurses began to take over and we felt safe in the knowledge that nothing more would be done to any patient until morning, Pauline sank back on to her pillow and, with her rosary beads threaded through her fingers, thanked God for His infinite goodness.

The night nurses, watching her at prayer, agreed among themselves, 'She's a little saint, that one.'

# OPERATION

ILAY IMMOVABLY bound to my hip frame with leather straps. Wearing a white operation gown, a waterproof cap on my head and thick, woollen socks on my feet, I had never in my whole life felt so warm. I lay still and afraid, with my forearm covering my eyes.

Sometime during the night they had brought me in from the veranda. I was awakened by the jerk as the night nurses pulled my bed into the back of the ward and drew screens around me. Then I had to suffer the shame and horror of the rubber tube being pushed into my back passage and warm, soapy water being poured through a funnel and into my bowel, filling me to bursting point. I had known this done to others, enjoyed and even joined in the sniggering and rude jokes that were made to add to the torment of the unfortunate one who was getting it. I never imagined that such a thing would be done to me, believing until the moment came that I was too good for such treatment, and anyway, I was in the best of health, apart from the one bad hip. It would never be my misfortune, I had firmly believed, to need an operation. The nurses had surely picked on the wrong patient.

I questioned them in an urgent voice but they replied cheerfully, 'No mistake, m'dear. It's yourself we want. This is to help your wound to heal, that's all.'

That's all! Did they think I was stupid? I kept my face

covered until it was over, asking no more questions, for fear of the truth.

After my body had poured out its waste, I lay awake working it out for myself. I had been in Cappagh for a whole year and was not so easily fooled. The truth was that my leg was not improving. It was worse, as a matter of fact. One abscess had taken its course, leaving me with a deep, open wound in my thigh, which still oozed pus into the thick dressings that were applied and changed each day. At a new spot I could feel the pain and tightness that told me another abscess was developing. But it would take more than a single enema to clear that up – twenty aspirations more likely, unless it had been decided that the leg had gone too far and would never get better.

We all knew about the Johnny who had had his leg cut off because it was so bad nothing could be done to cure it. He would have died, it was said, if drastic action had not been taken. Enemas were given before operations to empty you out before they made the cut. There was no other reason that I knew of to be sticking tubes into back passages. 'Jesus, mercy! Mary, help!'

After the morning prayers Sister Finbar's kindly face appeared around the screen. 'You're not crying, are you?' she said. I could not bring myself to answer, but from beyond the screens in the next bed, the eager voice of Kathleen O'Donnell explained in a rush, 'She had an enema, Sister, in the middle of the night, and she's crying with the shame of it.'

Sister Finbar bent down close to me. Her crucifix brushed over my hands, and I could smell her clean, starched linen. 'Look at me, Rosemary.' She spoke softly so no one else could hear, and lifted my arm away from my face. 'Do you remember what I told you about always trusting the doctors and nurses?'

'Yes, Sister.'

'If you were told to drink ink, you should do it because we know what's best for you?'

'Yes, Sister.'

'Even if it's a question of eating up all your sago!' She gave a little chuckle, and I nodded my head in sorrowful resignation.

'Well, then,' she went on, as if the problem had been solved and I need have no more worries, 'don't you know very well that we would not do anything to you at all, unless it was going to help in making you better. You're having your tonsils and adenoids out today.'

'Oh, thanks be to God,' I cried out with relief. 'I thought it was my leg, like the Johnny.'

'Now why would we be operating on your leg?' the Bar's voice became suddenly sharp.

'Because it's gone all bad.'

'Indeed it has not, and you should not be listening to any of those stories going around. Your leg will soon start improving, I promise you. You are doing very well. Now, don't be worried about the old tonsils at all. You will be better off without them. When you wake up this evening you'll have a bit of a sore throat and we'll get you some ice cream. Rest now, until they come for you, and ask Our Blessed Mother for strength and courage. She will never let you down.'

I closed my eyes and began a prayer of thanksgiving. Having the tonsils out was better news than I had feared, but even so, it was bad enough. I still had to face the nose-bag, which was our name for the anaesthetic, and so my fears quickly returned and my prayers took on a greater urgency. As I prayed I felt a stirring of the air above my head, and I heard my Mummy whisper, 'I'm here, darling, there is nothing to fear.' Then the trolley was there to take me to an unknown part of the hospital. My frame was lifted on to it by nurses wearing long, green gowns and masks on their faces. 'Are you coming for a spin?' said one.

'What nurse are you?' I asked.

'I'm Nurse Crown,' she said, lifting her mask for a moment to give me a cheery smile. 'You know me, don't you?'

'Oh, yes.' Of course, I knew Nurse Crown. She was one of our favourites. She worked in the theatre, and whenever she came with the trolley, she was great at getting at least a smile out of the one going for an operation. At other times, she would breeze through the ward on her way to or from her duties and always had a song or a joke on her lips, to which we responded willingly, reaching out to her because it seemed to us that she loved us all. 'But I didn't recognise you with your face covered,' I said, clutching her hand.

'We're going for a little jaunt,' she said. 'Come on now, we'll run all the way.'

Fast indeed they trundled me out of the ward to the shrill sound of the bell, high on the wall of the ward, blaring out the signal from the theatre to *Bring the patient – now!*

Down the back corridor we sped, out on to a covered walkway and in again to a long passage with walls of green tiles. The sounds of the veranda faded into the distance and were then cut off completely as the trolley moved smoothly through the double doors of the operating theatre. Lifted up again by many hands, I was moved sideways on to a flat table and a brilliant light shone hotly down upon me.

When I awoke I was back on the ward, in my own bed. Sister Finbar was there again, telling me how good I had been. My throat was on fire, and I saw and heard everything as though from far down inside a tunnel. Struggling against an overpowering smell of ether, I lifted up my head and tried to speak.

'What is it, child? Is there anything you would like?'

'I want my daddy,' I croaked.

'Never fear,' said the Bar confidently. "Your daddy will be here on Sunday, first off the bus.'

# SATURDAYS

ON SATURDAYS, THERE was no school, and no doctors came to disturb our contentment. We were kept busy all the same, getting ready for Sunday. Sheets were changed, heads washed and fingernails cut, too short to be any use for scratching. If, when the nurses had finished with us, we pleaded hard enough, they would move our frames to one side and leave beside our heads, on waterproof squares, the basins of water in which we had been washed. Then for an hour or more we washed our ribbons and doll's clothes, rubbing bars of clean-smelling soap round and round between our hands to make suds. Joining thumb and forefinger into a ring, we blew out huge bubbles which soared, gloriously coloured, up into the sky as far as the Johnnies' veranda and, if the breeze was gentle, over the altar itself.

'Mine's the biggest!'

'Ahhh . . . it's burst!'

'Mine's still going strong!'

We vied with each other and cheered our bubbles on, promising each other prizes of sweets or biscuits when the visitors came next day to replenish our stocks. We borrowed and bartered for coveted possessions.

'I'll give you my picture of Saint Francis for that handkerchief.'

'I don't like Saint Francis. He's too brown for my liking, and the handkerchief has gorgeous flowers on it.'

'God forgive you for saying you don't like a saint.'

'I didn't say I didn't like him . . .'

We operated on soft-bodied dolls, cutting into their bellies with blunt-ended scissors, poking out morsels of stuffing with knitting needles and painting over the slits with dabs of crimson lake from a paint box, which was exactly the colour of mercurochrome. We covered the wounds with bits of gauze, held in place by strips of sticking plaster begged from the dressings trolley. Other dolls were attached to cut-out models of hip and spinal frames, with proper, slotted-on footplates, which we cut out from the stiff covers of writing pads. During those games of hospital Marjorie rested, out of harm's way, in the locker under my bed.

Voices were lifted in unselfconscious song, nurses and patients teaching each other the words of old favourites: 'I'm a rambler, I'm a gambler, I'm a long way from home . . .', 'The Hills of Donegal', 'Moonlight in Mayo' – the songs of Delia Murphy, Bing Crosby and the Andrew Sisters. The voices of the Johnnies wafted over, sometimes singing but more often yelling and cheering as a football was headed or thumped with fists from bed to bed.

While we Biddies adorned ourselves with medals and scapulars and folded lace-edged handkerchiefs into the pockets of our clean gowns, birds swooped down on the veranda. We knew them all by name – willy wagtails, yellow hammers, finches and starlings – and showed no fear or surprise as they alighted on our bedheads, to watch our activities with cocked heads, or gathered on the floor in noisy groups to fight over fallen morsels.

The birds taught us more than any teacher could about the changing seasons. We got to know their ways and watched their comings and goings. In the autumn, we had seen the departure of the swallows, flying in formation to warmer climes, leaving the bare trees to the sparrows and crows. The crows were always with us, whatever the season, raucous and bad-mannered. Every morning they flew out in a body from behind the altar, as though on urgent business, and returned in the evening to rest in the winter trees. We replied to their squawking with equal racket and chanted in unison at the late stragglers, 'Ye're late, ye're late, ye're late for ske-wel. Ye'll get the cane, ye're late for ske-wel.'

As the weather grew colder, we had welcomed our warm flannel gowns and extra blankets and begun to think about Christmas. With the coming of spring, we delighted in the return of the migrating birds, for they brought with them the promise of sunshine and, before too long, liberation from our winter covering.

There was hardly a child among us who, having passed the four seasons of a year in Cappagh, could not recognise the leaves of all the trees that grew around the hospital. As they began to fill the trees and bushes all around us, Wastras would bring in branches and sprigs for us to handle and trace into our drawing books: shiny beech, green in summer, polished brown or scarlet in the autumn; hairy elm, recognised by the uneven way the leaves were joined at the stem; the spread-out fingers of the sycamore; the wavy oak leaves with acorns attached, like little boiled eggs in their cups. Grimly, Wastras told us, 'There are hardly any oak trees left in Ireland, since Queen Elizabeth had them all cut down to build her ships.'

The lighter evenings brought everyone a new lease of life, and we played on into the lengthening shadows of evening. Groups of off-duty nurses came down from the nurses' home and crossed in front of the verandas, to play camogie in the field behind the altar. In short gym slips, with their hair tied back with ribbons and slides, many of them looked like schoolgirls, far too young and good-looking to be grown-ups.

'Isn't it grand to see their hair!' we exclaimed with delight.

Johnnies whistled and howled at the sight of them and marked their passing with 'Da-dada-da, da-dada-da, da-da-da-da, da-da-da-da,' like when Laurel and Hardy were on at the pictures.

The nurses took no notice as they hurried towards the bushes that would shield them from our curiosity. Once they reached the field, we saw only quick flashes of their black stockinged legs through the high bushes, but the sound of their enjoyment and the thwacking of ball on stick mingled harmoniously with our own babble of contentment.

'We want to forget about you kids when we are off duty,' they would say the next day, when we poutingly reproached them for not waving.

When all had gone quiet, if enough light remained, I would reach into my locker for one of my two precious Christmas books. One was called *Where the Rainbow Ends* and was a story of two children who get lost in a forest and are in great danger of being devoured by a terrible dragon, with flames coming out of his nostrils, but are saved by Saint George, who in his shining armour arrives in the nick of time, slays the dragon and carries them home on his white charger to their grieving parents.

The other book was called *Peter Pan in Kensington Gardens* and that was about a boy who flies out of his nursery window into the park, where he comes upon plants that have faces and hold conversations with each other. They explain to him how they all come to life after the human beings have all gone home. Wearing only his nightgown, Peter flies up into the trees to sit on high branches among the chattering birds.

Now and then, Peter goes back to peep through the window of his house and is pleased to see his mother asleep, with a tear of sorrow trickling down her cheek. He will return to her, he thinks, when he has grown tired and seen enough of the wide world, but when that time comes, it is too late. The window is barred. There is a new baby in his cot, his mother is smiling with new happiness and has forgotten that Peter ever existed, so he flies off again with a heavy heart, never to return.

By now I had read both books many times and had become a good reader. I would sometimes read aloud to Eileen and Pauline, which at first they enjoyed, although they were very particular. If a certain chapter took their fancy, they liked to hear it many times, but if they took against anything, they would not even listen to the end and were ignorant enough to yawn and fall asleep. After a while they voiced their objections and said they were fed up with my kind of stories.

'I never heard tell of a Saint George,' Eileen said one time.

'He was English,' I explained.

'An English saint? Is it coddin' me 'ou are?'

'And the other one, that Peter Pan,' Pauline added tremulously, 'is far too sad.' With two against one, the books had in the end to be put aside. Instead, we took turns at reading from our school primer – *Stories of Ancient Ireland* – which we had to learn for Wastras. The other two read slowly, following the words across the pages with hesitant fingers. But the stories were worth waiting for, as they were full of goodness and glory and there were pictures of beautiful princesses called Maeve and Grania and Deirdre, who wore richly embroidered cloaks and bands of ribbon braided through their sun-lit hair. This was how the book began:

> *Erin long ago was the home of great deeds and noble lives. When its name is heard, in its sweet Gaelic form, on the lips of our children, our hearts are touched. Our minds travel back a thousand years to the Golden Age of the race . . .*

Before long, we had learned the whole book off by heart and believed in every word of it. On schooldays, Wastras would listen to us reading and tell us with great feeling in her voice that Ireland was in those times, still was and always would be the island of saints and scholars.

# THE STAFF NURSE

I F ANYONE WAS to ask us who, of everyone in Cappagh, we were most afraid of, we three would most probably have said, all together, 'Staff Nurse McGinty. No doubt about it!'

The staff nurse was tall and thin. Her uniform was a white coat like a doctor's, with buttons down one side, and her starched veil stood out stiffly to the width of her shoulders, marking her out as a very senior person, who was easy to spot from a great distance. We often heard the nurses complaining in low voices about her strictness, but they would also admit, grudgingly, that when McGinty went to town on her day off, she looked only gorgeous in her good navy suit with the pink blouse and her hair brushed out around her face.

That was a sight we never saw, although at times, if she was not busy, she would spend time with us in a good-humoured way and even turn her head to let us look up under the veil to admire her nut-brown hair, which she kept pinned up in sausage-like curls, all bunched together at the nape of her neck. That did not mean that we could take liberties with her. Oh, no! Most of the time, she ruled us with a stern face and was easily aggravated. Her voice then would come at you like a shot from a gun and everyone jumped to obey her instructions. We kept a sharp eye out for her all the time for fear of being caught doing something that would spark her off, and we sighed with relief when she left through the swing doors at the end of the day with 'Goodnight, children!'

Nurse McGinty had a habit of hovering with her arms folded while our beds were being made, to check that we were lying in our correct positions and had not been scratching our wounds. When my bedclothes were turned back, she pulled up her sleeve and thrust her arm down between my legs. 'Always check', she would instruct the nurses, 'that the coccyx is in line with the central bar of the frame.' Mine never was, and she would say I was the bane of her life as she pulled on my cords and straps, sometimes slapping any bit of bare skin she could get at to bring home, once and for all, the lesson of obedience.

'If you want your body to be all twisted up for the rest of your life, it's no skin off my nose,' was the kind of thing she would say, and her words would give me a stab of fear through the heart, for fear of what might happen if I did not obey her in all things.

On one occasion, her vigour in tying me down caused blood to ooze through my bandages, and when these were stripped away, two deep cuts were discovered where the sticking plaster had sliced into my leg. These were painted with iodine, which made me cry out with the pain. When the leg was bound up again, two windows had to be left in the strapping, so that these new wounds could be watched and regularly dressed. Nurse McGinty never said she was sorry, and we all agreed that as she was the nurse who most often did the aspirations, she was the main cause of everyone's crying pain.

But on that occasion we had the satisfaction of seeing her punished. Nothing could be hidden from the Bar, who, after examining my leg, said in a grave voice, 'The child will carry the marks of those cuts to her grave!'

We didn't hear what was said to Nurse McGinty about it, but we did see her going off duty in a great huff, disappearing through the swing doors without a word to anyone.

'Wouldn't you wonder,' Eileen remarked, 'at the way that nurse gives out to us all the time but is as nice as pie to the visitors?'

It was true. When my father came she was all charm, as if I was her favourite patient. 'A lovely girl,' Daddy called her, 'and a superb nurse.'

He was shocked when I told him about the cuts, and although I think he only half believed me, he said he would rather be lying there himself than see his little girl go through so much. But he would not have it that the nurse was to blame for my misfortune. 'She has to be strict', he said, 'to get things done properly.' And he urged me again to 'be a soldier'.

Nurse McGinty also supervised the meals, making sure that we ate up every scrap on our plates. 'There are millions starving,' she would remind us. Happily, I had lost my dread of the sago days, due to my arrangement with Eileen. I only had to wait until she had cleaned her own bowl. While waiting, I would stir my portion about as though getting ready to eat, mixing in the splash of jam that floated on top until I had a thick, purple mess. Then, when Nurse McGinty was far off down the veranda, Eileen would thrust her empty bowl towards me and, quick as a flash, we would make the exchange.

One day we were caught out. The nurse wheeled around too soon, as though suddenly remembering something that stopped her in her tracks. I saw her veil winging its way towards us and pulled back my hand too quickly. Eileen's empty bowl fell to the floor, where it wobbled loudly for a few seconds before coming to rest.

Nurse McGinty took in the situation at once. 'Is there no limit to your slyness?' she said, and pinching my nostrils together, she shovelled heaped spoonfuls of the hated frogspawn into my gasping mouth.

Hours later, after I had thrown up the sago, I was still retching at the thought of it. It had come back with force, spreading itself all over my hair, my gown, my pillows and blankets, and sticking my fingers together. Nurse McGinty, also badly splattered, rushed away to change her uniform, leaving two junior nurses to clean up the mess.

'That was my worst nightmare come true,' I said furiously to Eileen, 'more horrible than anything that has ever happened to me in my whole life, and it's all your fault! You are never, never going to play with Marjorie again.'

Eileen did not have a word to say in her own defence. She just turned her head away and covered her eyes with her arm.

# WAR!

I F IT WASN'T for my brother Paul, we would hardly have
known there was a war on. It was mentioned every
day, of course, on Radio Éireann, but the news, if we
heard it at all, was only about faraway places which had
nothing to do with us.

Paul cycled out to Cappagh every Wednesday, his half-
day off school. He wore his Belvedere cap and blazer, and
I felt proud of him and the admiring way the others
looked at him. After removing his bicycle clips, he fished
from his pocket the special gift which I came to expect –
a pot-bellied model of one of Snow White's seven dwarfs.
He brought one every week until I had them all: Doc,
Dopey, Sneezy, Sleepy, Happy, Bashful and, last of all,
Grumpy.

'Hello, Paul,' a chorus of Biddies greeted him as he
rode through the gates. Blushing, he returned the
greeting with a general wave of the hand. Sister Finbar
came out for a quick word, asked for news of his mother and praised him for his devotion. 'There are not
many boys would give up their time,' she said. 'Enjoy
your visit now.'

Paul brought us news of the war, which to me anyhow
was much more interesting that what we heard on the
wireless. He explained that Hitler, who was completely
mad and cruel, was whipping the German people up into

a frenzy and intended to take over the world, getting rid of anyone he did not approve of. Winston Churchill, on the other hand, was a good man and a brilliant leader, who was well able to deal with Hitler. There was no doubt, Paul said, about who was going to win the war and a jolly good thing, too, because if the Germans won, the whole world, including ourselves, would be enslaved. That gave me a terrible vision of being whipped and kept in chains, but I believed everything that Paul told me and took comfort from his assurances, because he was so clever.

The funny thing was though, Wastras thought the exact opposite to Paul. She said that the British were by no means as good as some ignorant people thought, that England was not a Catholic country, so where was the call for wanting them to win the war? What good would that do for Ireland? And she didn't seem to think there was any great danger in Hitler being the winner.

Paul then explained that a lot of Irish people hated the English because of things they had done to Ireland in the past, and even though thousands of Irishmen were away fighting in the British forces, Ireland as a nation had refused to take sides in the war with Germany. Opinions differed, he said, and to avoid bad feeling, it would be best for me to keep my mouth shut about the English, especially when the teacher was listening.

One day, Paul brought with him his school annual, *The Belvederian*. It was crammed with pictures of good-looking lads, in teams or class groups or, if they had won something, sitting on their own, holding silver cups. There were photographs, too, of the school opera, *The Pirates of Penzance*, in which Paul was in the chorus of policemen and had a false moustache on him. Others were dressed as pirates and the younger boys played the parts of the girls, with wigs and lipstick on them, so you could hardly tell that they were boys at all. Paul sang all the songs to me. He knew them off by heart, and he bent down close to my ear and glanced over his shoulder, to make sure no one was laughing at him.

> *For I am a pirate king.*
> *Hurrah! Hurrah for the pirate king! . . .*
> *And it is, it is a glorious thing . . .*
> *To be a pirate king.*

'Sing another one – and another,' I demanded, for I could not get enough of those songs with their lovely tunes and funny words. Such songs were never heard on the *Hospitals' Requests* programme. In no time at all I had all the words in my own head, and from then on sang them out loud to impress anyone who would listen.

> *Let us gaily tread the measure*
> *Make the most of fleeting leisure . . .*

As I took the music into myself and collected week by week my seven dwarfs, I also learned what was going on in Europe, according to Paul. He told me it was all a terrible worry to our father, who got up at six o'clock every morning to hear the latest news and couldn't bring himself to speak to the German couple who lived on our avenue. Of course, I was altogether on Daddy's side and prayed secretly for the British to win the war.

'I'll take you to the college opera every year when you come home,' Paul promised, and he left *The Belvederian* with me to enjoy for a week or two.

We passed that book from hand to hand, rubbing our fingers over the pages as we examined every face and memorised the names listed under the photographs. We all had our favourites among them and dreamed of romance.

# War!

*I am a courtier grave and serious,*
*Who is about to kiss your hand.*

When after a while Paul asked for his book back, I took it from under my pillow, reluctant to part with it. When Paul saw the dog-eared state of it he was very upset.

'It's all covered with greasy marks and you've broken the back of it! You must learn to have more respect for books. It's no good any more, you can keep it now!' Red-faced, he jumped on his bicycle and rode off at high speed.

'Paul gave out to ya.' Kathleen O'Donnell couldn't wait to put her oar in.

'He did not.'

'He did so. I saw him, givin' out to ya, an' his face all red.'

But Paul did not stop visiting me, an answer to prayer for which I was truly thankful, for I felt sick every day with the pain of his anger. The next week he was there again and did not even mention the book. He told me instead about Spitfires and Messerschmidts and German bombers that flew over London every night. People were being killed in their thousands, he said, and their homes blasted to smithereens. There was not enough food to go round, so I should count myself a lucky girl to be in such a safe and happy place.

And it did seem that apart from the prayers for peace that we offered up every day, the troubles of London and the war were very far away from Cappagh and hard to believe in.

Until . . . Early one morning when it was hardly light, we were awakened by night nurses and day nurses, all dashing around together in a panic, pulling the beds back into the wards, closing over the doors and bolting us inside. Sister Finbar and Nurse McGinty shouted out orders, and when we were all safe inside, they knelt side by side on the floor and began to recite the rosary in loud, supplicant voices. Without a moment's hesitation, we gave the responses, picking up the urgency, even though we were only half-awake.

Suddenly, the sky overhead was filled with terrifying noise, as though some wild beast was tearing up the fabric of the sky with bared teeth. It was so loud, we thought the building would collapse around us, and shaking with fear, we pulled our blankets over our heads and put fervour into our prayers.

'Mother most pure, Mother most chaste, Mother undefiled . . .' the Bar's voice could just be heard, reciting the litany.

'Pray for us. Pray for us. Pray for us,' we beseeched, keeping it up until at last our prayers were heard and silence fell. It was all over in a few minutes, and afterwards the deafening silence was gradually filled with the comforting sounds of an early breakfast and the everyday din of our lives was restored. On his next visit, Paul brought the news that a Spitfire had chased a Messerschmidt across the Irish Sea and hounded it to its destruction in the Wicklow hills. It was an isolated incident and did not mean that the war was coming to Ireland. There was nothing at all to worry about, he said. Mr Churchill had everything under control.

Wastras offered prayers for the repose of the soul of the German pilot.

# A Surprise for Eileen

SOON AFTER OUR own taste of the war, Sister Finbar came along the veranda with a letter in her hands. I reached up to take it.

'It's not for you at all,' she said, playfully smacking my hand. 'It's for you, Eileen, from your mammy.' The envelope was already slit open. The Bar unfolded the single sheet of lined paper and read:

> Dear Eileen,
> I hope this letter finds you well, as we all are here, thank God. Your Daddy is going to England to join the Army the sooner the better for there's nothing for him here. He will be catching the Mail Boat from Dún Laoghaire and will call in to visit you on his way past
> . . .

There was more, about the brothers and sisters and neighbours, who were asking for her and praying for her speedy recovery. But all that paled in the light of the big news, that Eileen was to be visited by her father, whom she had not seen for a year or more.

'He doesn't be working much,' she told me, 'but I'm sure he will bring me something – a doll or maybe a box of Galtee cheese and, of course, I'll share it with 'ou all.'

'Why don't you write him a letter', I suggested, 'and send him a list of things you would like?'

89

Eileen looked doubtful. 'I don't think . . . I mean, there's a lot of children at home,'

But she agreed it was worth a try, so from that day on, Eileen wrote to her father every single day and made lists of the presents she would find most acceptable. The letters were torn up every evening because she was not satisfied with her handwriting, because she had thought of a better list to write the next morning, or because maybe it was best to leave the choosing of the presents to her father. That way, she said, she would get a nice surprise.

After receiving her mother's letter, Eileen talked about her home more often. The memories awakened about her brothers and sisters made her smile and laugh, but it was clear to me that there was hardship in the family and that her father would have little to spare for the buying of presents. In my prayers, I gave thanks that even though our family was not as rich as Mummy would have wished, my daddy was at least able to afford the bus fare to visit me and would never dream of coming empty-handed.

On the subject of the expected visit, Eileen became serious. 'I don't know how it will be, or what I'll say to him,' she said. 'Da's not a great one for children. It was all right if he was workin', but the times he'd be out of work and hangin' around the house, Mammy wouldn't be speakin' to him, and we'd all be watchin' ourselves for fear of gettin' in the way of his hand. Then he'd go out in a temper, and we'd all be talkin' together and crackin' jokes, and Mammy would sit down for a smoke.'

Here Eileen would pause to give an imitation of her mother smoking – putting two fingers up to her mouth and sucking in air with a desperate, gasping sound, which made us laugh.

'Then 'our man'd come in with a fish or a rabbit, and

they'd be speakin' to each other again. Sometimes we'd see him standin' with the men at the end of the street, and if we passed by, he might give us a salute, but then again he might not, and we'd wonder, was he able to tell one child from another at all?'

Weeks passed, and every time the bus was heard arriving at the gate, Eileen twisted herself around and with her double-jointed arms lifted up the weight that swung from her head. Then she was able to raise herself high enough to watch the bend in the drive for a new face to appear among the visitors. She was not sure, she said, that she would even recognise her da – it had been that long. Only for his hair, which was red, exactly like her own. 'As soon as I see the hair, I'll know him,' she said.

'Is that him, I wonder, that skinny fella!'

'No, that's Mary Kelly's father.'

'What about that one there, in the brown coat. Look, he's wavin' his arms.'

'No, I don't think so, but I'd have to see him without his cap.'

'Ay, take yer cap off, Misther.'

Eileen read her letter over and over until she had the words off by heart. She kept it under her small, flat pillow where she could easily get at it. It soon grew dirty and ragged from all the handling and, in time, fell to bits.

Still, her daddy did not come.

It was many weeks later when the night was disturbed by the sound of weeping. Not a child but a man. A distraught man, completely out of control, sobbing into his daughter's bedclothes as she lay in her upside-down world, waiting for her presents. He arrived after dark, on his way to catch the boat to England in the morning, a man from a country place going to war and asking at the convent door to see his daughter for the last time.

A nun gave him a cup of tea and gave out to him for his lack of faith in God's goodness. Every day the children offered prayers for peace, she told him, and sure, he might not be killed at all but would be home again in no time, a better man for the experience. It was most unusual to let visitors in at night, but since he had come a long way and still had far to go, she would allow him to go down to the ward and see his daughter, just for a few minutes. The child had been looking forward to the visit, but he must promise to be very quiet and not disturb the other children.

Eileen was gently called awake. Her bed was drawn into the back corner of the ward and surrounded with screens. The man thanked the nurses for their trouble, calling them angels. They found him a chair to sit on and went away, keeping their distance, even though they were perplexed by such a rare occurrence and unsure of how to deal with it.

Without speaking a word, he suddenly put his head into his cupped hands and began to sob, crying out his farewell to the world and his last confession to the children of Blessed Imelda's ward. We began to stir in our beds, some of the little ones crying out in fear of the terrible sound. Pauline and I stared sleepily at the space where Eileen's bed should have been and, for a few moments, could not place the noise we were hearing.

The night nurses looked at each other in bewilderment. 'Merciful heaven, what are we supposed to do about this?'

In the morning, when the screens were removed, Eileen lay with her face turned to the wall, as still and as petrified as a new patient or one who is sleeping off an anaesthetic. Sister Finbar held her hand after the morning prayers and spoke quietly in her ear. Wastras gave her bed a miss when doing her rounds with the school work. Only Kathleen O'Donnell had the audacity to mention the events of the night.

'Was that yer daddy, Eileen? He was upset, wasn't he? Had he drink taken, I wonder?'

'Shh!' The nurses ordered her to be silent and leave Eileen in peace, but in her delight at finding herself beside the one she regarded as the liveliest patient of all, Kathleen kept a close watch for the smallest sign of Eileen coming out of her shell to provide the answers to her burning questions.

'Are y'all right, Eileen? Don't be cryin' now. Offer it up.' Eileen lay still and silent.

For me, too, it was a quiet morning without the sound of Eileen's voice, and as I waited for her to be returned to my side, I found myself thinking about the war and how Eileen's daddy was surely going to be killed in it, for it was clear to me that he would be hopeless at defending himself and would be likely to stop the first bullet that came his way. Not that Eileen would miss him all that much. She had so few good memories of him and, indeed, had not even been sure she would recognise him when he came. Still and all, you would have to pity him and could never forget the awful sound of a grown man crying his eyes out, or the scuffling and the urgent whispering as he was led away by shadowy figures, who had been sent for to get rid of him. Lying awake in the silence after he had gone, I thought I would rather eat sago every day of the week than see my daddy in such a bad way.

With a great rush of pity, I made two important decision: first, I would allow Eileen to play with Marjorie for a whole day, and second, I would beat the daylights out of that Kathleen O'Donnell, if ever I got close enough, for if ever anyone deserved a belting, it was her.

At last, Eileen was returned to the veranda and in a little while uncovered her face. I gave her my most friendly smile and with Marjorie dressed in her finest, ready to be handed over. Slowly, Eileen lifted herself to the edge of her mattress, and even though she could not bring herself to look me in the eye, she reached for my hand.

# EASTER

A T EASTER, THERE were more presents and chocolate eggs from Sandycove.

'This one is from the Bowers next door.' Daddy called out the names of the givers as he produced each one from a large bag. 'This one is from Miss Mac of the sweet shop and, oh! Look at this! Guess who sent you this wonderful thing!'

'Uncle Sam,' I said at once.

Uncle Sam was not really my uncle but a neighbour, who passed our house every day on his way to and from his office. I would watch for him in the evenings, just as I did for Daddy and he always stopped for a little chat with me, raising his big hat and laughing with real enjoyment at my way with words. Often, he would give me a bar or two of chocolate out of the machine in the railway station, and from the time I came to Cappagh, he had never let a special occasion go by without sending me a present.

This time, Daddy said, he had surpassed himself with a cottage made of chocolate, as big as a pan loaf. Its doors and windows were marked out with sugar piping and surrounded with pink icing roses and green leaves. Everyone who saw it made sounds of wonder.

'It's a work of art,' said Sister Finbar, when she came to chat to her favourite visitor. But her face was serious as she took Daddy by the arm and led him on a slow walk along the veranda. They were gone for what seemed a long time, and I began to worry that she might be giving him some bad news about my hip that I wasn't supposed to hear.

When at last he came back to me, Daddy looked very serious. 'You are such a lucky girl,' he said, 'with so many people sending you lovely things. Why don't we give this cottage to little Kathleen, who has no visitors.'

I could not believe what I was hearing! Even though I was well used to sharing my presents by now, the thought of being so generous to that one inside the ward, who was nothing more than a pest to us all, was too much to ask.

'I'll give her one of the small ones,' I said grudgingly, but it was no use. Daddy had made up his mind. 'No,' he said, 'she is a long way from home and she should have a special Easter present.'

I could tell from his voice that it was useless to argue, and even if I managed to get the better of him, the Bar would surely get to work on me and win in the end, since it was, I guessed, her idea anyway that I should sacrifice my best Easter box to someone who was worse off than myself.

Kathleen, for some reason unknown to us, had lately become everyone's special pet and so, in our eyes, became more aggravating than ever. I could not understand it, but with a pout on my face, which no one heeded, I made the big sacrifice, consoling myself with the thought that I was storing up special grace for my immortal soul.

'Be sure to tell Uncle Sam what you made me do,' I instructed Daddy as he went in to see Kathleen.

'Do you know what, Misther,' said Kathleen, accepting the cottage without surprise, 'I'm goin' home next week, so I am!'

'Are you really? Well, well, that will be a great day in Poolaphuca!'

'Ah, stop yer foolin' now, sure that's not a place at all, only one of yer daft words. Don't ya know very well that I live in Limerick. It's a terrible long way from here, and I'll be goin' in an anubulce at eight o'clock in the morning. It'll be dark by the time I get home. Isn't it great news altogether?'

Her eyes were bright with joyful images, and as she spoke, her skinny little fingers sank into the chocolate. The roses fell away from the sugar trellis, a hole appeared in the wall and the cottage caved in under her hands before she had even given herself a chance to admire it.

'How could she be going home?' we asked each other in disbelief. She had not had her feet on the floor since coming to Cappagh, and she had been there longer than the rest of us. Mr Macauley was always knocking on her knees with his silver hammer, but her legs never jumped or even quivered, but lay still on the bed like two white, mottled sticks.

We told her out straight that we didn't believe her, but Kathleen swore by all the saints that it was true. 'That I may be struck dead this night!' she said, with her hand on her heart. 'The Bar came to me and she sez, "Would you like to go home, Kathleen?" "I would, of course," sez I. "Good girl," sez she, "we'll let your mammy know."'

Of course, you couldn't believe a word that Kathleen said, but very soon the Bar confirmed that it was true; Kathleen O,Donnell was going home!

'But she's not better!'

'She's not able to walk!'

'No, she's not better yet,' Sister Finbar agreed, 'but we'll get her a chair, and she will do better, please God, when she is at home with her mammy.'

It made me feel sick with envy to hear the way Kathleen boasted her news to everyone who passed her bed. Anyone would have thought she was more important than the rest of us put together, just because she was leaving us behind and going off to what she kept saying was a far better life. Thinking about the happiness that lay in store for her, I was all the more furious with my daddy for making me give away my beautiful chocolate cottage.

The day Kathleen went home, she was put into a brand new dress that looked far too big for her, with a pattern of flowers and a real lace collar. A pink satin bow was tied on to a tuft of her hair and held in place by many hairgrips. Around her neck hung a big bunch of miraculous medals, some on fine chains, some on ribbons, to ensure that Our Lady would go with her and protect her. These were gifts from nuns, nurses, even a few older patients, who on hearing the news sent down presents from the top end of the veranda, even though they had never laid eyes on her. A going home was, for everyone, a cause for celebration. Even the girls had clubbed together and given her a rosary in a gilded box, and they all spoke to her in sweet, petting voices, saying they were delighted for her sake but, all the same, sorry to see her go.

Kathleen was carried into the ambulance and propped up with pillows on the stretcher bed. After her went a wheelchair and two cardboard boxes, one packed to the brim with neatly folded clothes and the other full of toys and story books from Saint Anthony's. As she waved her goodbyes, Kathleen's face was miraculously made beautiful by her perfect happiness.

Nurses and girls gathered in a group around the open doors of the ambulance. Wastras, in the midst of them, turned away suddenly and we saw tears in her eyes. Sister

Finbar was half inside the ambulance, making sure that Kathleen was comfortable and had not forgotten anything. Everyone was smiling and wishing her well, as if she had been the most popular patient in the whole hospital.

As for ourselves, we were always pleased to join in any kind of celebration, even if we didn't understand the call for it. So we added our voices to the cheering, waved our hands and lifted up our heads, to get a last look at our tormentor.

'Goodbye now! Goodbye! God bless and keep you and don't forget to pray for us.'

'I'll not forget a single one of ye,' Kathleen promised, 'an if I'm ever round this way again, I'll come and visit ye all.'

'Three cheers for Kathleen O'Donnell!'

'Hip hip – hooray! Hip hip – hooray! Hip hip – hooray!'

Only a few weeks after we had seen her off, on a day that no visitors were allowed, a stout woman in a tight coat and headscarf came around the bend in the drive. She approached our veranda on squeaking shoes, her cheeks burning under the curious eyes that watched her all the way across the open space.

'Is this Blessed Imelda's?' she asked at the first bed she came to.

On being told that indeed it was, she unclipped a large, shabby handbag and took out a bundle of holy pictures. Licking her thumb as she went, she moved from bed to bed, giving each one of us a picture. She gave no explanation but moved quickly, as though in a hurry to get her business over and done with. We accepted her offering without question and turned the picture over to read with amazement the words printed on the back.

The woman had nearly reached the end of our veranda and was about to continue on to the Little Flowers when she was seen by Nurse McGinty, who shouted from afar in her sharpest, most heart-stopping voice: 'And where, may I ask, did you come from? This is not a visiting day.'

The woman dipped her knee in a kind of genuflection. 'I'm Kathleen O'Donnell's mother, ma'am, may the Lord have mercy on her.'

'Oh, Mrs O'Donnell,' Nurse McGinty's voice changed to a softer tone, and she took the visitor by the elbow. 'Why did you not let us know you were coming? Such a long way for you. Come with me now, Sister Finbar will want to see you. What have you there? Oh merciful heaven. Nurse!' she raised her voice again, the way she did in times of emergency and a junior nurse came running. 'Take those pictures up from the children at once!' She bundled Kathleen's mother out through the back door of the ward and left her to wait in a quiet room with a cup of tea until Sister Finbar could be found.

My picture, which I managed to hold on to, showed Jesus, looking like a five-year-old child but still lying in his crib. He had flowing, golden curls and his eyes were as blue as marbles. His hands were spread out, palms upwards, with beams of radiant light coming out of them. Underneath was written in gold, *'Suffer the little children to come unto me and forbid them not.'*

I turned the picture over and read:

*Pray for the soul of Kathleen Philomena O'Donnell*
*Born on 25th January 1932 – Died 1st May 1941*

This was followed by the words of the hymn we knew so well and in which Kathleen's voice, not long ago, had put the rest of us to shame.

*Oh Mary, we crown thee with blossoms today,*
*Queen of the Angels and Queen of the May.*

We were very quiet for the rest of the day, thinking about Kathleen, who didn't seem half so bad now that she was dead. We asked no questions about the way she had died or why, when she had been full of life only a short while ago. But Sister Finbar came to talk to us about it after the visitor had gone home.

'It was God's will,' she said. 'We did everything possible but couldn't make her better. But now Kathleen is a saint for all eternity. To give a little soul to God is a wonderful thing, and that is a great consolation to her mammy and all of us.'

Then, since the truth was out, she gave us back our memorial cards and led us in a decade of the rosary, adding the prayer for perpetual light to shine on Kathleen's soul.

When all the lights had gone out, we were still exchanging our thoughts and were in agreement that Kathleen must surely have her crown of golden roses by now. We believed what we had been taught: that when you die young, there is no question of purgatory, even if you have been a pest and a nuisance in life, but straight up with you to heaven, all sins forgiven, in the arms of the Blessed Virgin.

'I wonder,' said Eileen, 'would she still have her hump?'

I thought about that for a while before answering, 'Oh, I wouldn't think so. But then again, it's hard to imagine her without it.'

Eileen said, 'Sure you couldn't be perfectly happy, even in heaven, with a hump on your back.'

'You could so,' Pauline retorted, 'because everyone who goes to heaven has to be in a state of grace, and if you were in a state of grace itself, you wouldn't be jeering at them that has something wrong with them, sure you wouldn't?'

We had to agree that this made sense.

'Shh! Quiet out there, you three,' the night nurse called out.

Pauline, for a change, was determined to have the last word.

'Why would you not be perfectly happy?' she hissed in a loud whisper. 'Wouldn't you forget you had the hump, if nobody ever mentioned it?'

# BOMBSHELLS

IN THE LATE spring of 1941, an announcement on Radio Éireann blared out across the verandas. A bomb had fallen on Dublin, in an area of the city called the North Strand. Thirty-seven people were killed and many more injured. Homes and shops were destroyed, leaving an enormous pile of rubble from which bodies had to be dug out.

In Cappagh, all those who had contact with the children were told to make light of the incident, but since it all happened so close to home, we could feel the tension in the air. The faces of the staff wore grave expressions as they talked quietly among themselves, with much shaking of their heads. To us, they spoke in lighter tones, but they could not alter or take back what we had heard with our own ears on the wireless.

It was a tragic mistake, Sister Finbar told us, hoping to quickly put our minds at rest. No one wanted to harm the Irish people, she said, certainly not hospital patients. By the grace of God, it would never happen again, so we were not to give it another thought, except, of course, to remember the dead and their families in our prayers. That was nothing new. We prayed for the dead every day of our lives.

But if Sister Finbar thought that was the end of it, she had another think coming. She had reckoned without the visitors, who were full of their own versions of what had happened. You couldn't put a stop on people's tongues, Nurse McGinty was heard to say, for the bomb had brought home to the people of Dublin that, neutral or no neutral, 'In the midst of life, we are in death,' and, 'There, but for the grace of God, go we all.'

On the first visiting day after the calamity, one woman ran all the way from the bus, outstripping everyone else to be first to arrive at the veranda. With raised voice, she started telling us all about the terrible fate of her first cousin.

'I was only talkin' to her the day before it happened, and the next I heard, she had been blown to bits. There wasn't a scrap of her found. God alone knows what went into the coffin!'

'I say there, come here to me.' Sister Finbar stormed into view with her veil flapping and her face scarlet with rage. She pulled the woman out of our hearing, and we watched her giving out a long lecture, with her finger wagging, while the woman hung her head in shame.

Paul told me the details of the bombing in a low whisper. It was no mistake, he said. Hitler had deliberately ordered it, meaning to warn the Jews on the South Circular Road that he knew they were there and could not hide from him for ever, that he'd catch up with them as soon as he had the war won and that would be the end of them. But, of course, that was just ridiculous, because we all knew that Hitler hadn't a hope in hell of beating the British.

When she had finished with the troublesome woman, Sister Finbar came for a few smiling words with Paul and, as always, praised him for his devotion.

Another time, when we had nearly forgotten about the bomb and were feeling safe in our beds again, I was horrified to hear that a shell had been fired on Dún Laoghaire, very close to my house. One explanation was that a German U-boat had sneaked into Dublin Bay with the intention of blowing up the mail boat, because it was carrying people to England to join up with the British Forces. Others, who still found it hard to believe that the Germans could want to harm the Irish – and they so obliging as to stay out of the war – were of the opinion that the U-Boat had only wandered off course into Irish waters and that the shell had been fired wildly by our own Local Defence Force, who had panicked in their fear of an invasion. Whichever version was the truth, the torpedo had missed its target and veered towards Rosmeen Gardens in Dún Laoghaire instead. Paul went down on his bicycle to see what damage had been done, saw the huge crater in the middle of the road, but was able to report that the houses were still standing and no one had been killed.

At the end of each day, when the nurses had tidied up our beds and settled us down for the night, Marjorie, too, was put to sleep in the locker under my bed. She lay in there with her eyes closed and her dress smoothed down until the next afternoon, when school and the serious matters of the day were done, then she was brought out and laid at my side. One busy evening my bed was overlooked in the changing shifts of staff, so Marjorie was still with me after the day nurses had gone. This was a rare chance for secret play, and as soon as quietness fell over the verandas and Pauline was asleep and breathing noisily through her mouth, I whispered to Eileen, 'Are you awake? Come on over!' Even though Eileen, too, had been nearly asleep, her hand shot out immediately, as I knew it would, for she never missed a chance to be close to Marjorie.

We were quite certain we would not be disturbed unless someone called out for attention, but we were not cautious enough. A night nurse, hearing the sound of our two beds crashing together, crept up on us and we were caught. 'The cheek of you two,' she said in a shocked voice, as if she had never before come across such wickedness. 'Playing a game, if you please, at this hour of the night!'

Eileen had seen her first and gave warning in a loud whisper. 'Quick, hide Marjorie!' My frame was still perched precariously at the very edge of the mattress and there was no time to do anything about that. All I could do was to push Marjorie down under the bedclothes and lie still with my eyes tightly closed, hoping that the nurse would content herself with telling us off and go away.

'Just look at the cut of you,' she went on. 'I know you're not asleep. I've been told to keep an eye on the two of you. You are just getting too big for your boots.'

'I only whisht we had boots on us to be gettin' too big for,' Eileen said in the hope of making her smile.

'Stoppit! You know very well what I mean. Settle down now, please,' she said, softening up a little. 'I'm late going off to my supper.' As she spoke, she yanked the beds apart, lifted me up by the bars of my frame and dropped me in the middle of the mattress.

The sound of Marjorie's face being crunched under the weight of a hip frame was more terrible to me than all my imaginings of war, the pain that took hold of me worse by far than aspirations or the cuts of sticking plaster. I opened my mouth and screamed once, twice, three times at the top of my voice. The silence of the night was broken, anxious murmurs came from wakening patients and even the distant babies could be heard crying in their cots.

A second nurse came running. 'Is it an air raid or what?'

'Nothing that serious, only this bold girl getting hysterical,' and raising her arm, the first nurse struck me smartly across the face.

A moment later, I threw back the bedclothes and revealed the devastation beneath. Then it was the nurse who lost control of herself, and throwing up her hands she burst out crying.

''ou're after killin' Marjorie,' said Eileen, who was the only one able to speak.

'Let's get rid of this first,' said Sister Finbar, peeling a squashed rasher sandwich off my chest, 'then I'll tell you some wonderful news.'

As I wakened to the sound of her voice, I stared for a moment, then remembered that something so terrible had happened I was never going to be happy again. I turned away from her glowing face, unwilling to hear her words. What could she have to say that would comfort me? And anyway, I did not want to be cajoled out of my misery, least of all by the Bar, who worked so hard at talking us into or out of all our moods.

The guilty nurse had done her best to repair the damage to Marjorie's head. She spent nearly an hour patching the pieces together with strips of sticking plaster, pulling the hair forward to cover the worst of the cracks, but she only made matters worse. After all her efforts, the beautiful blue eyes, lids and lashes all of a piece and stuck on the prongs of a leaded wire, still rattled around loose inside Marjorie's skull, there being no hope of sticking them back into their shattered sockets. I could not bear to look at her, and in the end all the nurse could do was to wrap my precious Marjorie in a towel and put her back in my locker.

I could not be consoled, and after they had tidied away the broken pieces, the nurses left me alone, but I could hear them, every so often, creeping along to see if I was still crying. I pretended to be asleep but stayed awake for a long time, trying to pray, all the time losing my place and having to start again. 'Hail Mary full of . . . Blessed art thou . . . Perpetual light shine on them . . .'

I was still awake when the nurse who had hit me came back from her supper. She touched me on the arm and offered me a fat rasher sandwich, which at any other time would have been a great treat and a sign of favouritism, all the more exciting for being eaten in the middle of the night.

I knew I would not be able to eat it, but I accepted it with thanks, for I could see that she was nearly as upset as I was myself. She kept saying she was sorry for hitting me and would, of course, pay for a new doll.

'Don't you know by now,' I cried, 'there's not another doll like Marjorie in the whole world?'

I fell asleep at last, the rasher sandwich clutched in my hands, and the next thing I saw was the Bar's face close to mine and heard her saying, 'Wonderful news altogether. Do you not want to hear? The very best thing that could possibly happen.'

'Am I getting off my frame?' I asked weakly.

'Even better than that! You'll never guess.' She held the sandwich away from her clothes and was in no way annoyed about it, although we knew how she disapproved of the nurses bringing us food from their dining room.

Guessing that she had not yet been told about my tragedy and knowing that I would have to find the words to tell her, brought on the tears again. I said with a broken voice, 'Marjorie is destroyed.'

'Ah, not at all. She can get a new head on her when we have the time. Come now, why would you be crying over an old doll when you have a brand new baby sister!'

# THE NEW SISTER

'A SISTER? HOW? When was she born? Will my daddy bring her out on Sunday?'

'Hold on now, indeed he will not.' The Bar threw back her head and laughed. 'She is with your mammy in the nursing home, and the two of them will come together, as soon as they are strong enough.'

'What is her name?'

'Oh, something very unusual. What's this it is now?' The Bar thought for a few moments, staring into space with a frown. 'It begins with "S" – Septa, Seraphina, I didn't quite catch it on the telephone. Your daddy will give you all the details when he comes. Now, you must write your mammy a letter to say "congratulations", and I will find a little something from Saint Anthony's for you to send to the baby. Isn't that wonderful now? Didn't I tell you? Thanks be to God!'

She was right again. The whole day was filled with new questions racing through my mind and with the writing of the letter. I hardly had a minute to be upset about Marjorie, lying dead in the locker, though I did remember to tell Mummy in an easygoing way, so as not to be upsetting her when she was so busy with the new baby.

> *Dear Mummy,*
> *I hope you are well as I am myself, thank God. A nurse has smashed Marjorie's head . . .*

Wastras made me start again. 'Don't be so selfish,' she said, 'bothering your mother with that, at a time like this. You are to say how thrilled you are with the news of the baby and ask after her health and strength.'

Many rough copies were made of the letter. My hand grew hot and damp from squeezing the pencil and my fingers were aching long before I got it right. I had to leave out all my questions because they would have made the task even longer.

> *Dear Mummy,*
>
> *I hope you are well as I am myself, thank God. I am delighted to hear about the baby and am offering a novena to the Little Flower for you and her, that you will both get strong soon and come to see me for a visit. Saint Teresa is everyone's favourite here and Teresa is my favourite name . . .*

Wastras said that would have to do, but only because she had a bus to catch. She would post it for me, she said, but when she had her back turned for a minute, I scribbled quickly on the back of the page, 'When you're coming, will you bring me a bottle of Californian Poppy perfume, please?' then quickly stuck the envelope down before Wastras could find out that I was asking for something, like a beggar.

I could hardly wait for seven o'clock to come, for then I would be free to say anything I wanted to my own mother, without interference.

'Mummy,' I whispered when the moment came, 'it's really great about the baby and I'm only delighted, but I'm sorry to tell you that Marjorie is destroyed and my heart is broke.'

Mummy turned slowly around from the crib, where the swaddled infant lay on a mattress of hay, a cow and a donkey keeping her warm with their breath. Mummy lift-ed her veil away from her face and turned her eyes of pity upon me.

'My poor darling,' she said, 'you must be very brave now until I bring the baby out to meet you. Think about home now and all the wonderful times we will have together, never to be parted again.'

It was hard to imagine that from now on there would be another girl in our family. I tried to imagine her but it was impossible. I had never seen a newborn child, only kittens, and they had pink noses and were blind and too delicate to be handled, although the mother cat was able to carry them in her mouth without doing them any harm. My cat Snookums had kittens one time, five or six of them, all different. They had to go, of course, but I was allowed to keep one of them, pure white she was, and I loved her so much that I used to carry her about under my jumper.

I asked Nurse McGinty what size a newborn baby would be.

'Tiny,' she said. 'She could probably lie on the palm of your hand.'

I repeated to Mummy in our evening talks that Teresa would be a lovely name for the baby, or Therese, whichev-er she preferred, after the Little Flower of Lisieux. I longed for Sunday to come when I would get a letter from her, telling me all I wanted to know. I prayed that she would be better from her long illness, so she would be able to cope with all the extra work and having to stay up all night to mind the baby. She had always pitied the mothers of big families, and I thought how hard it was that a baby had been sent to her at a time when she was not feeling her best and I was not there to help her.

'Babies come out of their mothers' belly buttons,' Eileen informed me.

'Oh, that's dirty,' I protested.

'Honest to God,' she said. 'Down the country cows do push out calves, and people do the same with babies. Babies definitely come out of their mothers' belly buttons.'

I was sickened to think of my mother having to go through anything so rude.

'You know nothing,' I retorted. 'Animals are quite different from people. With human beings, the doctor brings the baby to the nursing home in a black bag.'

'And where does the doctor get it from, tell me that?'

I could not think of an answer, so Eileen called out to a nurse, 'Ay, Nurse, where exactly do babies come from?'

'From under the goose-gob bush, of course,' she told us with a dead-straight face.

In Cappagh, the mention of a new baby made everyone smile, from Sister Finbar down to the girls, who paused in their sweeping to congratulate me on the great news.

I would never be short of someone to play with, they said, when I went home. 'Much better than a dolly,' they said.

Even Mr Macauley looked pleased. He nodded his head approvingly and said it was a good thing for the mother. So it was, I thought, since Mummy had been without my company for so long and the baby would be sure to cheer her up.

I was delighted, too, when Wastras lingered by my bed, her face all smiles as she told me all about her sister's little boy, who was two years old and her godchild.

Sunday came at last, and the moment Daddy arrived we bombarded him with questions. I wished that the others would shut up and let me have my private say, but the baby, it seemed, was everyone's news.

'How is she gettin' on now?'

'Who does she look like?'

And most of all, 'When is she comin' out to see us? Will ya bring her out soon? Ah, please, bring her next week.'

'Soon,' Daddy promised. 'As soon as she is able to travel. You know we can't bring her on the bus, she is much too precious, but Uncle Dick will lay on his company car, as soon as he can. The baby will arrive in great style.'

Soon – soon – soon! The same old answer that we got to our most important questions. We knew by now that the word 'soon' only meant that no one had an answer, maybe wouldn't tell even if they had. We just had to put our requests into our prayers, then wait patiently for God to provide the answers in his own good time. Still we kept up our pleading, changing to a new set of questions, which might have an immediate answer.

'What size is she? Has she hair on her?' And oh, of course, I nearly forgot to ask, 'What is her name?'

'Listen,' Daddy said, raising his hands in the air, 'the answer is "yes" to everything. She looks like a little stewed prune. She looks just like you and her name is Stephanie.' At that, we fell silent. Ste-fa-nee? What sort of a name was it at all? We had never heard the like of it. Nurse McGinty exclaimed, 'Oh that is lovely – so unusual.'

But Pauline announced with great solemnity, 'Sure, there's no saint of that name,' which worried me a bit but gave the grown-ups a laugh.

Marjorie was wrapped up in a brown paper parcel and carried away under Daddy's arm. 'I'll take her to the dolls' hospital,' he said, 'and she will have a new head. You'll never know the difference.'

Before leaving he wrote a note to the nurse who had done the terrible deed, telling her not to worry any more

and ending with: '. . . but you will have to be more care-
ful, when the real dolly comes visiting, because if anything happens to her, there will be real trouble.'

We put the matter of the baby's name to Wastras, who
said suspiciously, 'It sounds a bit Russian to me!' but
added that she would look the name up in a book she
had at home. The next day was able to reassure us. 'Of
course, there is a saint. Can anyone tell me who that is?
No? Why, Saint Stephen, of course – the first martyr,
whose body was pierced with a thousand arrows.
Stephanie is the female form of Stephen!'

This news came as only a small relief to me. I still
thought it a peculiar kind of name, especially the way
everyone was pronouncing it, at the same time, pulling a
bad face. Ste-fa-nee, Ste-fanny.

'But then again,' Pauline pointed out, 'a lot of saints
have unusual names, and I'm sure you'll get used to it.'

I was grateful to her for being so kind about my sister's
name, and I quickly came to the conclusion that even
though it was not my choice, the name must be beautiful,
because Mummy had chosen it.

# THE VISITATION

THE LIMOUSINE GLIDED slowly through the gates and came to a halt, right at the foot of my bed. The driver in his peaked hat jumped out and ran around to the back door. After a few moments of activity inside the car, Mummy appeared, pale and smiling.

She came towards me with outstretched arms and tried to put her arms around me, but seeing that my frame made that impossible, she took my two hands in hers and kissed me, many times, on my forehead and cheeks.

'Oh, my darling,' she said in a broken voice, and I saw to my great surprise that she was trembling all over, as if dying of the cold.

There were so many things I wanted to say to her. Even though I told her everything in our nightly chats, I still wanted to make sure that she had heard it all correctly, but at that moment I forgot everything except that she was here on the veranda, holding my hands and smelling of the powder and perfume I remembered so well.

I felt shy of her and said politely, 'Hello, Mummy, I hope you have your strength back.'

Mummy was wearing a dark, loose coat. She had a red velvet turban on her head and a scarf to match. The richness of the material made her look pure white, except for her lipstick, which perfectly matched the velvet. Under her coat, two enormous soft bosoms sagged down past her waist.

'You look wonderful,' she said, 'brown as a berry and your hair more blonde than ever!'

Still tongue-tied, I kept my eyes off her bosoms and said I was feeling grand, thank God.

'How I've missed you, my darling,' she went on. 'I think about you all the time and can't wait to have you home again. How I will spoil you!'

By this time, Auntie Molly had stepped out of the car and, with the help of the driver, approached my bed with the Moses basket containing the baby. Sister Finbar arrived at the same moment, her face alight, as if nothing in the world was as pleasing to her as the sight of them. After the joyful greetings, she lifted my frame to one side and picking up the swaddled babe laid her carefully down beside me.

Having been told that you could hold a new baby in the palm of your hand, the size of my new sister came as a surprise, but even though she was bigger than I expected, she was beautiful in every way. Her eyes were tightly closed and one little clenched fist was pressed against her cheek. I could feel the soft touch of her breath on my face and the delicate new smell of her in my nostrils.

'She has no hair,' I said. 'I thought she would have a bit of hair by now.'

Mummy laughed. 'Give her a chance,' she said. 'She is only one month old, and see, she has a little wisp.' She touched the baby's head with her finger, raising a feather of golden down.

Pauline, passing by on her afternoon walk, was led forward by Sister Finbar to have a peep at the baby and present a gift. Proudly she held out to Mummy a picture of

the Sacred Heart, sewn on to a small, heart-shaped cush-
ion of white satin, which was embroidered with pearl
beads and red sequins. 'It's blessed by the priest,' Pauline
said, touching the baby's cheek. 'If you pin it on her jack-
et, or inside the basket, she will be kept safe from all
harm.'

The baby's fist opened and clutched on to Pauline's
stiff finger. 'They do all love me, the babies,' she said
proudly. 'I do visit them below there every day and make
them smile. They are all little dotes!'

'Well, I think that's wonderful. Thank you, Pauline.'
Mummy accepted the offering and tucked it down the
side of the basket. She was smiling as she said in an aside
to Auntie Molly, 'Little dotes! Don't you love those
Dublin expressions!'

Sister Finbar then picked up the baby in her arms and,
moving aside her crucifix, rested the precious bundle
against her chest. The baby's eyes flickered open for a
moment and a strange little smile touched her mouth.

'She's smiling!' I cried. 'Look at her, she's smiling at
me!'

'And why wouldn't she?' said the Bar. 'Aren't you her
big sister? You will be a very important person in her life.'

Then she carried Stephanie up the veranda and down
through the ward, walking at the same slow pace as when
she was saying the prayers. She stopped briefly for every
nurse and girl and bent over the beds, allowing every
child a peep. But no one, apart from myself, was allowed
to kiss the baby.

'I hope you are keeping to our pact,' Mummy said. I
told her with some surprise that of course I was and that
seven o'clock was the most important time of the day. I
would never let a day go by, I assured her, without telling
her everything that happened to me, didn't she know

that? She squeezed my hand and said we must keep up the habit.

At last the visit came to an end, and I was so tired from all the excitement I was glad for them to go, so I could relive the day in my mind and practice for the next visit, when I hoped I would find better words to say.

I clung to Mummy's neck as she kissed me goodbye. 'When will you come again?'

'As soon as ever I can.'

'Next week?'

'Well, maybe not next week but soon, I promise – and, of course, I'll be thinking of you every night – on the dot of seven . . .'

Gently she unlocked my hands and climbed back into the limousine. As it slid away I could see the bright red turban, the pale face smiling out from the back window. She kept waving her hand until the car disappeared around the bend in the drive. I raised up my head and watched the gleaming roof skimming fast along the top of the hedge towards the road. Then it was gone.

'Did she really come,' I asked myself, 'or did I only dream it?'

Everyone who passed my bed all evening added more to my happiness.

Wasn't it a wonderful day for you? You saw your Mammy! Thanks be to God!'

'Oh that baby! She's only gorgeous!'

'And the weather stayed fine for your visitors!'

Eileen got fed up with all the attention I was getting. 'Anyone would think you were a fillum star!' she said.

There was a new doll for me and fancy biscuits in a tin. Sister Finbar gave permission for our three beds to be brought together for a bit of a party. We each got a tri-angle of Galtee cheese and three biscuits of our choice before the tin was snatched away and doled out to all the patients down the length of the veranda.

After we had eaten, we gave our full attention to the new doll. She was smaller than Marjorie but her hair was longer. You could plait it! Not only did her eyes open and close but they turned from side to side as you moved her around, like the eyes of a living person. As Mummy had pointed out when she gave it to me, the doll was exquis-itely dressed, with a full outfit of clothes, including an overcoat and hat. There was no doubt about it, we all agreed, even though she was on the small side, my new doll was, like my sister, perfect in every way.

'She will be called Teresa,' I said, which, in a way, made up for my disappointment over the oddness of my sister's name.

As darkness fell, we were still going over the events of the day in drowsy whispers, breathing in the luscious scent of Californian Poppy in which we had doused our-selves. We fell silent and began our private prayers. It was long after seven o'clock, and for myself I could think of nothing more to pray for, now that I had seen my Mummy and the baby. But I thought of the story Wastras had been telling us about the good leper who was cured by Jesus – how he had been the only one out of twelve to go back and say 'thank you'. Well, the whole day had been like a miracle for me, so I kept repeating, 'Thank you, God. Thank you, Mary,' as I drifted off to sleep.

I was nearly gone when Pauline asked an important question.

'What did youse two pray for?'

Eileen answered drowsily, 'I prayed for long . . . curly . . . hair, like Baby Jesus.'

I did not want to talk any more, but I did feel kindly disposed towards Pauline, who had given a present to the baby and because she hardly ever got any visitors, so I asked her patiently, 'What did you pray for, Pauline?'

'Well,' came the reply, 'do you know them black, shiny shoes, the kind the Irish dancers do wear, with the silver buckles on them?'

'Oh them are grand,' said Eileen, wide awake again, 'and the long white socks that go with them, with ribbons at the knee!'

'Patent leather,' I said.

'That's it,' Pauline was delighted. 'Patent leather shoes! That's what I prayed for.'

We crossed our arms over our chests, the way we had been taught to do, in case we should be taken in the night. One last effort was all that was needed to end a perfect day. I took the lead:

'May the Almighty and Merciful God grant us pardon, absolution and remission of all our sins.'

'Amen,' said the other two.

# ANOTHER CHRISTMAS

THE SUMMER PASSED, and as autumn turned into winter, there was no great news to highlight our days. We accepted with little complaint the slowness of our progress, the pain of our damaged bodies and the treatment, which was just as hard to bear. We were, after all, especially favoured by God, and so we lived our days in faith and hope, while waiting patiently for our separate miracles to happen.

I spoke to my mother every evening, but her face was often blurred and I was no longer sure how to imagine her. Sometimes I dreamed about being in a place that felt like home, and she would be sitting at the breakfast table in her blue velvet housecoat, reading *The Irish Times*. At other times, she was more like a heavenly figure floating above my head and speaking into my ear with a more gentle voice.

Eileen and I had now been in Cappagh for more than eighteen months, Pauline even longer. We were the three most senior patients on Blessed Imelda's veranda and we considered ourselves nearly grown-up. This being so, we began to take a greater interest in the Little Flowers, whose lives seemed, from the little we could see and hear, to be far more interesting than ours. Eileen talked longingly about moving up there. 'We'll surely be moved in the New Year,' she would say, and I would quickly reply, 'If we're still here.'

Meanwhile, another Christmas was approaching, and by the beginning of December, I had to accept that, in spite of the many prayers I offered for that special intention, I would not be spending it at home. It was no use being disappointed. It was God's will.

As Wastras often told us, 'Every little prayer you say is heard in heaven, and there is always an answer – but sometimes the answer is No!'

So, I threw myself into the preparations, which from the first day of December began to gather speed. It was, after all, the birthday of Baby Jesus, and everyone, staff included, was caught up in the festive spirit.

'Big girls you may be,' Wastras said, 'maybe not quite big enough to move up the veranda, but big enough to help with the Christmas decorations.'

Hundreds of blue, yellow and silver shapes had to be cut from rolls of crepe paper and woven into chains and baubles for the adornment of Blessed Imelda's ward. There was contentment in the task, and as the garlands grew out of our hands, we joined in as Wastras sang to us in her clear, lilting voice and the world seemed altogether brighter, with good times still to come.

Eileen was still praying for a dolls' hospital. 'I'll get it this year for sure,' she said. 'It will be exactly the same as Cappagh, with verandas and little beds with dolls in them. The dolls will have arms and legs that you can bend any way you like. That way, I'll be able to put them on hip frames and spine frames and weights and pulleys, anything I like. There will be little trolleys with chubes and funnels for enemas and needles and . . .'

'Who is going to give them to ya?' I interrupted her, thinking that if such a toy existed, I would be the first to hear of it and my daddy would be sure to buy it for me. 'Not Mr Kenefick, that's for sure, nor the real Santy either.'

'Mammy will send it in a parcel. She told me in a letter.'

'You haven't had a letter.'

'I have so.'

'You have not. Don't be telling lies. You haven't had a letter or a visitor since your daddy went to England.'

'That's what you think. I don't tell you everything.'

'You do so.'

Seeing that her story was weak, Eileen covered her eyes with her arm, to show that she had nothing more to say on the matter.

We were playing hospital that day, our favourite game. I was Mr Macauley and Eileen was Mr Carney, the man who came to measure you up for frames and splints. She was cutting out a hip frame for an unimportant doll, suitable to be used as a patient. Marjorie was the mother, arriving with presents and showing concern for her child. After the doll was bandaged on to the frame, Mr Carney was no longer needed in the game, so Eileen became Nurse McGinty and we had a discussion about the seriousness of the patient's affliction and the treatment she would have to receive.

'Well, now, Nurse, this patient will have to have her knee fused. I noticed on the X-eray that she has a confusion of the tibicular, which is very serious indeed. She won't be able to go home for at least five years. Tell me now, is she keeping her food down?'

'I'm afraid not, Doctor, and her bowels have not opened for six months. I think we'll have to stick a chube down her troat and another one up her bum.'

'Oh my poor child,' I spoke for Marjorie, bending her over to kiss the patient's face and speaking in a heavenly kind of voice.

If I was truthful I would have had to admit that Marjorie was no longer beautiful. Her new head looked too small for her body, and although her complexion was the same delicate pink and cream and she still had her fine clothes, her new eyes were brown, her hair the colour of tow. Next to the perfect little Teresa, with her living eyes and glossy plaits, Marjorie looked – it pained my heart to admit it – ugly and common, like Titchy of the Buildings. But those words would never pass my lips. I could never hurt Marjorie's feelings by letting her know I had gone off her. I had made up my mind to go on treating her the same as before – with love and praise – never allowing a word to be said against her or letting her be used in our games as a patient. After all, a mother didn't go off her own child just because something happened to spoil her perfection. But there were whole days now when Marjorie was left alone in the locker, and I tried not to think about her as I regained my pride from Teresa.

Eileen, as always, had to come straight out with the truth, as soon as the parcel from the dolls' hospital was opened. 'She's aww-ful-lookin!' Seeing the look of dumb misery on my face, she did her best to cheer me up, though I suspected that behind her comforting voice, she was really quite pleased. 'Don't cry, Rosemary – haven't you got Teresa to take her place?' For all the comfort she was to me, she might as well have said, 'It serves you right and I'm glad she's ruined! Now you're no better than the rest of us!'

'No one will ever take Marjorie's place,' I had screamed, thumping my fist again and again on the mattress, wishing it was Eileen's head. 'Didn't I tell you before, many times, there – is – no – doll – in – all – the – world – half – as – good – as – Marjorie!

'And anyway,' I added, to get my own back on her, 'there's no such thing as a dolls' hospital.'

For several days leading up to the feast, we were given only the most necessary treatments. No doctors came and the nurses, for the most part, smiled on us and encouraged our exuberance. The garlands were hung and we practised our carols to sing at the Christmas Day mass.

But for all the excitement, the day itself did not at first live up to my expectations. It was not like last year, when a trolley had to be brought to carry all the beautiful presents that came from Sandycove. They had all felt sorry for me then, being in hospital for Christmas, and I had felt so important, sharing my presents with the other patients and getting plenty of praise for it. Now, with the passing of another year, I felt I had been not exactly forgotten but was no longer such a special case, and my pile of presents was much smaller.

There was no sign of Mr Kenefick, at last too old to play Santy. Instead, it was one of the nurses who came dressed up in the red outfit and had us roaring with laughter at her performance. She was far too skinny for one thing, and although she did her best to put on a deep voice, she herself found it hard not to burst out laughing.

The rest of the day passed happily. We ate our fill of sweets and enjoyed our new toys

But the best news was still to come.

# PANTOMIME!

THE NEWS WENT around that in the New Year that a pantomime was to be put on in the Little Flower ward, which had been chosen because it could take the largest number of beds. We could hardly believe our ears when we heard that Johnnies were going to be wheeled over to see the show, and for maybe a couple of hours we were all going to be together under one roof. We talked about it day and night, and mixed with our excitement was a thrilling sense of nervousness. It was one thing to shout and hoot at Johnnies from afar but quite another to see them close up, maybe even have to talk to them.

Ann Kelly lived a fair way up the Little Flower veranda. She was thirteen years old and, in our eyes, a very senior girl. We never saw her up close, but she was a large presence in our lives just the same. She had a fat face that would stand out in any crowd, and hardly a day passed when we didn't hear her, shouting or bawling out in her strong Dublin accent the words of street games and the latest songs, which she always managed to learn off by heart before anyone else.

When Ann Kelly heard the news about the pantomime, she set up three raucous cheers, to let the Johnnies know the kind of welcome they could expect. The Johnnies cheered and whistled in return, and every day it seemed, whenever there was a pause in the activity, Ann Kelly would set up a new swell of sounds and signals, to which we followers added the full pelt of our voices.

Eileen said she wasn't one bit worried about meeting Johnnies, and if she got the chance she would tell them all the jokes that she had ever heard from my daddy. Pauline, on the other hand, was horrified. During all our excited talk she remained pale and quiet and was all the time drawing her blankets in closer around her body.

'It's not right', she said, 'for boys and girls to be mixed together in the same ward.'

'It'll be all right,' Eileen spluttered, 'as long as you don't have to ask for the bedpan while they are here.'

'It's like a madhouse,' Wastras complained, after being nearly deafened by an outburst of cheering. Removing her hands from her ears, she gave out to us: 'You are not to be making such a big thing about meeting boys, who are only young people like yourselves, for God's sake.'

She took her complaint to Nurse McGinty, saying there was no controlling us, that it was an unhealthy sign and we should be told that we could only go to the panto if we behaved like Christians. 'It's not that I begrudge them the fun,' she said, 'and some of those nurses are to blame. Imagine talking to eight and nine-year-olds about boyfriends, I ask you. They are all man mad!'

Nurse McGinty, who had never got on with the teacher, was pleased to disagree. 'And what kind of occasion of sin would they be in danger of,' she asked, 'and they all tied down to their beds?'

The main topic among the staff was how to fit everyone in. Large as it was, the Little Flower ward would not hold every single patient in the hospital. We discussed among ourselves who might have to be left out. Babies, of course, would be too young to enjoy a pantomime and might cry during the performance, so that let them out. Then, every ward had its share of very sick or gormless patients, who wouldn't know if it was Christmas or Tuesday, so they could safely be counted out. Some thought that those Johnnies who were nearly men would not be bothered with a pantomime, but Nurse McGinty, who seemed to be softened up by the whole idea, said, 'Everyone loves a pantomime, no matter what age they are. We'll manage. No one who is able for it will be left out.'

During all the talk about practical arrangements, it was a while before we got to thinking about the show itself. When we did, even Pauline cheered up and began to show some curiosity. 'I was never at a pantomime,' she said. 'I can't imagine what it will be like at all.'

I was able to tell her. 'It's a fairy tale acted on the stage. Girls dress up as boys and men act as funny old women called dames. They act the Mick and throw custard pies, an' all like that. There's a prince and a princess, there's singing and dancing and music played by an orchestra . . .'

'It sounds good, all right,' Pauline said cautiously.

In the Gaiety theatre in Dublin, the seats were rich and red, like the velvet of my dress. Gilded figures leaned out from curlicues on the ornate ceiling, like angels at the gates of heaven. Every seat was taken, upstairs and down and in the boxes at the sides of the stage. Happy families ate chocolates and clapped their hands with delight at the comical antics going on on the stage.

We sat near the front of the parterre, and from the moment the orchestra started up, my whole body quivered with the magic of it all. I longed to leap up from my seat, to dance and sing in the brilliant light and colour of

129

a fairy tale land, the land of bedtime stories, where good and beautiful people found love and lived happily ever after and the villains got their just deserts but in the end were forgiven, because they had made us laugh.

Jimmy O'Dea was the dame, and before he even said a word, the audience gave him a roaring welcome, for he was the most famous dame of his day and had only to cock an eyebrow, Daddy said, to bring the house down.

In the interval, as I swirled my ice cream around with a little wooden spoon, I announced, 'I'm going to be a famous actress when I grow up. Definitely!'

'Mind your dress now,' Mummy said, tucking a hand-kerchief under my chin.

A committee was set up to start the ball rolling. Full of light-hearted energy, two nurses and the junior house doctor went around with pens and note pads, rallying all levels of staff to put themselves forward for parts in the show. Those who agreed raced off every evening to attend rehearsals in the nurses' home. Some members of a musical and dramatic society came out from Dublin, generously giving up their spare time, to give advice and assistance in the production and stage management. The most important of these was Joe Holly, an experienced pantomime dame and occasional broadcaster on Radio Éireann. 'Weren't we lucky to get him!' everyone said. 'Isn't he very good, all the same, to be giving his time?'

The secret of a good pantomime, Joe Holly told the cast, lay in not sticking to the script. You had to be topical, he said, which meant telling jokes about anyone in authority who was used to getting respect. You had to get a rise out of them – Sister Finbar, for instance, or Mr Macauley. Could they think of anyone else? He would give them an example:

Question: When the Lord Mayor of Dublin dies, what will they do with his right hand?

Answer: Put it in a glass case in the museum and write under it 'That shook yez!'

The next most important thing was to get the audience involved as much as possible, choosing songs like 'Run Rabbit Run' and 'Daisy, Daisy', so that everyone – oh yes, nuns included – could all join in. Having a chat with someone in the audience and making them, in a nice way, the butt of your jokes.

We lay still and kept our mouths shut while our beds were being made so we would not miss a single scrap of gossip dropped by the pre-occupied nurses.

'Well, I grant you, Crown is a lovely girl, all right. She will make a lovely Cinderella.'

'I believe McCarthy was raging that she wasn't given the part.'

'I think McCarthy would have been OK actually. She may not have the high voice, but I hate Crown's carrotty hair.'

'Ah, but Crown has the voice.'

'She has, right enough. A wonderful voice.'

'And what about Casey for principal boy? Those legs! I'm sure she has them on upside down!'

It was not long before we noticed that some people were not speaking to certain others. The girls, in particular, were nearly all in a huff, which was bad news for anyone who needed anything picked up from the floor. No one was brave enough to stand up to them in their rage, for no one could bring themselves to be as rude and impudent as they were, with their back answers and the power they had, knowing that when it came to keeping the wards and verandas clean, they could not be done without. It was only when Sister Finbar was present that they behaved themselves. Then it was 'Yes Sister, No Sister,' as if they were the most kindly, obliging people you could find. Everyone else they ignored, whether or not they were to blame for the slight that had been done to them. They banged their brooms and polishers about, as if beating someone to within an inch of their lives.

All became clear when it was whispered that Joe Holly had suggested a special number, to be performed by the girls alone. He had put words of his own to an old Irish air. They were to be dressed in their caps and overalls and wave mops and brushes about in the air as they sang: *'We brush and scrub and sweep and clean . . . For we are the merry household team.'*

'Topical how are ye!' was the girls' answer to that. 'You won't see me in no pantomime. I wouldn't lower meself.'

'That's girls for you,' said Nurse McGinty.

# THE PERFORMANCE

THE PREPARATIONS BEGAN early in the morning, with the sound of sawing and hammering coming from the Little Flower ward as the handymen worked hard to build a platform for the players. We could hear the squeaks and clashes of colliding beds as space was made for the invaders, who would arrive from all parts of the hospital in the afternoon. As well as the thrill of a pantomime, we were filled with excitement at the prospect of seeing new faces, and although the waiting time was hardly bearable, we were kept amused by the laughter and raised voices of energetic staff, who seemed delighted with the diversion from normal duty and threw themselves into the spirit of the occasion. Even Wastras and Miss Riain, the senior teacher, having given up all hope of getting anyone's attention for the lessons, lent a hand wherever they could.

After an early dinner, which nearly choked us, Eileen and myself were among the first to be wheeled along the veranda. Pauline, as a small up-patient, would be squeezed in later on a chair. Beds were jiggled and nudged in an effort to fill every inch of space, and some of us yelped with the pain of sudden jolts to our bad limbs. Not that we cared, for this was a rare event, to be enjoyed to the full, and nothing – not even a bit of pain – was going to be allowed to spoil it for us. We revelled in the movement for its own sake, as much as in the reason for it, thinking it as good as the bumper cars at Toft's Amusements.

As we lay waiting and watching the activity, we recalled the night the aeroplanes went over, for not since then had there been such an air of confusion and urgency, which we had not, at the time, recognised as fear for our safety. That night had also been a highlight in our lives, to be talked about and savoured for ever more, for we now knew that a miracle had taken place and our lives had only been spared because of all the prayers that were said. And now the pantomime, which was going to be better still, better than anything that had gone before, and there was no danger in it at all unless, as Eileen pointed out, we were going to die from laughing.

Still bedecked with the blue and silver garlands of Christmas, the Little Flower ward was a grand sight to behold. Longer than ours by far, it was the domain of the big Biddies, some of whom we recognised by the sound of their voices but whose faces came as a surprise to us. The bigger they were, the more they looked on us with calm interest, and in spite of the disruption to their peace, many of them smiled on us with grown-up tolerance.

'We'll be comin' up here for good an' all, sometime this year,' Eileen said happily.

We had been given a place near the front of the audience, with a grand view of the stage. Only a few little ones were in front of us, and those who were not on spread-out frames were put two to a bed. Pauline, with a startled look on her face, was propped up on a straight chair against the wall.

When all was said and done, no one was left out who had a right to be there. In Blessed Imelda's ward, only four little Biddies remained in the emptiness. They would never know what they were missing. The Bar was there minding them and giving them treats from Saint Anthony's.

A stout lady visitor took a bow and sat down at the piano, which had been brought down from the nurses' home. She was wearing a long satin dress with a white, artificial flower pinned to the shoulder and another one behind her ear. She had a strong voice and kept shouting, 'Come on now, children, you know the words, let's hear you loud and strong: "Run, rabbit, run, rabbit, run, run, run . . . !"'

We sang shyly at first but soon warmed up and opened our throats, only to lose courage again as the rumble of wheels was heard and we knew that the Johnnies were about to appear. Then our voices collapsed like houses built of cards.

Small boys came in first, to fill the spaces reserved for them, their red counterpanes clashing with the abundant blues of our everyday vision. Along the full length of the ward, the glass doors that gave on to the veranda stood open, and the big Johnnies, last to arrive, were pushed head first into the openings, with their feet left outside.

I looked up as a huge red bed loomed above my head. My heart gave a lurch, and I had a sudden vision of the mail boat, thrusting its way through the mouth of Dún Laoghaire harbour. The Johnny in the bed was lying on his front, raised high on a reverse spinal frame, head in the air, big hairy arms folded in front of him. His bed-clothes were raised high on a tent frame to keep the weight off his legs, and the sheer bulk of him and his contraption filled the doorway nearly to its top and blocked out the light of the day. His bedhead came to rest against the side of my mattress, and I looked up from far below into the smiling face of a grown man who could, if he had a mind to, have reached down and patted me on the head.

The pantomime began with Nurse Crown, dressed in a ragged overall and crying because she was not allowed to go to the ball but had to stay at home and scrub the floors, while her two stepsisters went off in their finery to enjoy themselves and meet the handsome prince.

Crown's red hair was combed out loose and fell down past her shoulders in strong, crimped waves. You would wonder how she ever managed to get in all under a nurse's veil. She said a long piece about how cruel her stepsisters were and how weary she was of doing all the work. Then she began to sing 'Some Day my Prince Will Come' in the high lilting voice that came as no surprise to us, for we heard it so often as she went about her work. Like Wastras, she knew thousands of songs.

As soon as the song was over, Nurse Marr, a big woman, came on the stage wearing a nurse's cloak. She was stooping down as if she was an old crone but then straightened up, threw off the cloak and under it was wearing a net dress with tinsel pinned all over it and wound around her head. She waved a magic wand about, saying, 'You shall go to the ball.' Crown's rags fell off her to reveal that she was also wearing a gorgeous pink dress. We all cheered at the sight of that and had to be hushed down by Marr, forgetting for a moment that she was a good fairy, to get silence before she could say the most important line in the whole show. 'Hush now, listen to this: yes, you shall go to the ball, but you must be home on the stroke of midnight.'

The two artistes playing the Ugly Sisters were men, and one of them was Joe Holly. They wore daft costumes and their faces were plastered with clownish make-up. They strutted about, hitting each other with handbags and arguing in comical voices about which of them was the most beautiful.

'I'm going to marry the prince.'

'Y'are not! The prince will choose me, for sure.'

'Will we ask the children to decide? Which one is the most beautiful, children?'

We were nearly lifted out of our beds by the screaming din that rose up and the whistling of the Johnnies as we sent home the message 'Cin – de – rella!'

'Cinderella? Don't be stupid. Cinderella is only a scullery maid. You have to choose which one of us two the prince will fall in love with . . . come on now, say eeny, meeny, miny mo . . .'

We screamed out the words, but the two clowns kept getting their arms in a twist and could not get a result, so we had to recite the jingle all over again, and at the end of it they were still arguing the toss.

'I'm going to tell Sister Finbar on you.'

'Well, I'll get Sister de Montford on my side.'

They pelted us with sweets and told jokes about deValera and the lord mayor of Dublin, and we thought we would never be able to stop laughing and screaming, as one delight was heaped upon another.

For the ball scene there were eight dancers, dressed in traditional Irish costumes of green, white and gold. They took their places in a space left on the solid floor, because the stage would not have been strong enough for the weight of them. The pianist was joined by a man with a melodeon, and the dancers poised themselves, perfectly still as they waited for the opening chord, their faces solemn, their backs as straight as ramrods.

And oh, what a sight it was to see our nurses transformed into the dancing princesses of Éire long ago! With arms held stiffly by their sides, they made wonderful patterns of sound with their steel-tipped shoes, and the music of the land filled us all to bursting point. We clapped our hands and roared, 'More! More!' and the dancers obliged us for as long as they were able. Finally, breathing heavily from the exertion, they fell out of their sets, shook their heads and placed their hands over their thumping hearts.

After that, the story of how Cinderella got on at the ball and all the confusion over the slipper seemed a bit tame, although we had another good laugh when the Ugly Sisters were trying to get the slipper on over their stripy stockings, and when Crown and Casey sang their final song, 'Oh Love Is so Sweet in the Springtime', with their arms around each other's waists, they got plenty of whistles and cat calls, especially from the Johnnies.

'Shhhhhh!'

The noise died down as a column of nurses in full uniform filed silently through the only unfilled door from the darkened veranda. Some of them carried glowing lanterns, and they formed themselves into two ranks, one on the stage, the other on the floor below. A single chord was played on the piano and they began to sing, unaccompanied, making their own harmonies:

*Silent night, holy night –*
*all is calm, all is bright . . .*

The voice of the Johnny was so close to my ear that I could feel the warmth of his breath coming down on my face. The sound that he made was deep and manly, and it blended exquisitely with the treble voices of the nurses. Crown's high voice soared above all the rest, and the close-woven harmonies reverberated through the steel frame of my bed and all through the highways and byways of my strapped-down body. It felt like the playing of a huge orchestra, and suddenly losing all shyness of the Johnny's powerful presence, I wanted only to have my share of the perfect moment. I sang out the beautiful words and turned to look, for the first time, into his face. He had brown, merry eyes, a deep dimple in his chin and jet-black hair, combed back off his forehead in a oiled quiff.

*Sleep in heavenly peace,*

Our voices climbed heavenwards but Crown's was higher still,

*Sleep in heavenly peace.*

The beds began to thin out, and the sound of the carols gave way to the trundling wheels of the departing audience. My Johnny, for he had now become for ever mine, spread his arms out sideways and gripped the door frame, to help with the easing of his bed backwards out of the ward. Just before he disappeared, he looked down at me once more, and with a tender, sideways movement of his head, he winked his eye. It was as though we shared some kind of secret between us.

# Pauline's Trek

FTER THE PANTOMIME, the Little Flower's ward became more interesting to us than ever. We now had a real picture of it in our minds: the wider space of the ward and veranda, the glass wall at the end, with a view across the fields. We were charmed, too, to have been among the big Biddies for that unforgettable occasion, some of whom had welcomed us with friendly smiles, while others appealed to us just because they were so cheeky and full of themselves.

As another Easter approached, we three were looking forward to our ninth birthdays, and even though we knew that you had to be ten before you were moved up the veranda, that didn't stop us from a longing to be senior and somehow hoping that the rules might be changed for us. From where we lay, the big Biddies always seemed contented and busy with activities that we could only guess at, and we were easily distracted from whatever we were supposed to be doing on our own veranda by any flurry of movement or laughter up there. Wastras, more often now, lost her temper and raged at us for not paying attention to our lessons.

'Maybe you'd like to go up there for good,' she would say, 'and good riddance to the lot of you.'

'Oh, yes, please,' Eileen said. 'I'm sick and tired of all these young ones.'

'You just wait,' Wastras smiled her grim smile, 'till Miss Riain gets a hold of you. You won't get away with any nonsense, I can promise you.'

Her tone suggested there were terrible trials in store for us if we moved on but I liked the look of Miss Riain, and although her voice was often sharp and strict, I felt she could not be so hard on me as Wastras was.

Eileen took the warning with a laugh. 'I won't be afraid of Miss Riain,' she said, 'and I'll be glad to see the back of *her*.' She pulled a face behind Wastras's back.

Wastras was the one and only reason why I wanted to be moved, for I knew she did not like me. In her eyes, I was spoilt, English and had too much to say for myself. She never missed a chance to make me feel ashamed, criticising my way with words and the books I was given which, she noticed, never had Irish themes. Standing near my bed with her arms folded, she was for ever bringing up the subject of how badly the British had, for hundreds of years, treated the Irish.

'But I'm not English,' I tried to plead with her. 'I was only born over there. My Mummy's name was Molly Flanagan before she was married.'

Oh, yes, I could make her smile sometimes, but in the long run it made no difference to the unfriendly things she said in my hearing. So, I made a big show of joining in Eileen's praise of everything to do with the Little Flower's ward, and yet whenever I thought of being parted from Sister Finbar, I was filled with another kind of misery, and worst of all was the thought that I might still be in Cappagh when I was ten.

From time to time we tried, without much success, to attract the attention of the big Biddies, waving and calling out any names that we had been able to discover, mainly from the girls, for it was they more than anyone who most often crossed the invisible boundary line between the wards. At best, we were ignored or, if we became too persistent, called 'babies' by the nearest Little Flowers and told to mind our own business. We thought that if they knew us better they would get to like us, and one day we got the idea of sending Pauline up the veranda with messages of friendship.

'Go right to the top', we said, 'where the grown-ups are. They will have better manners.'

Pauline was scandalised. 'What if I'm caught? I'll be kilt!' But the thought of upsetting us was even more of a worry to her, and so it was settled. She would go on a Saturday afternoon when they would all be taking their ease and staff would be thin on the ground.

'On your way, you can get talking to Ann Kelly,' Eileen instructed her. 'I think she's about halfway along.'

'Sure, how will I know which one is her? I don't know what she looks like.'

'Folly the noise,' said Eileen.

Whenever Ann Kelly raised her voice, we went quiet and listened for the words of the latest songs, which she learned from her many visitors, who poured off the bus on Sundays.

> *I made ya look, I made ya stare – I made the barber cut*
>     *yer hair.*
> *He cut it long, he cut it short, he cut it with a knife and*
>     *fork.*

That became our chant for new patients when they had their hair cut for the first time.

> *Oh Doctor, oh Doctor, oh dear Doctor John,*
> *Your cod liver oil is so pure and so strong.*
> *I'm afraid of my life I'll go down in the soil,*
> *If my wife won't stop drinking yer cod liver oil.*

When we heard that one, we knew that a nurse was doing the rounds with the doses.

'Imagine bein' beside that every day!' Eileen said longingly.

The thought gave me no pleasure. Ann Kelly only brought back memories of Titchy of the Buildings, who I could still see in my mind's eye, swinging out of a lamp-post, poking her tongue out and saying, 'I don't like you, young one.' The last thing I wanted was to be put beside the likes of that.

'Ann Kelly is rough and bold,' was Nurse McGinty's opinion, 'and her songs are vulgar. I'm very glad I don't have to cope with her on my ward.' She was smoothing down my counterpane as she said it, and her words gave me comfort and a strong feeling that I was better off where I was, for Nurse McGinty had a lovely smell about her, and no matter how much she gave out, you always felt that she was a good, safe person to have in charge of you.

'Sure, they're all nearly grown up, those patients on the Little Flower veranda,' I pointed out. But nothing that was said could put Eileen off the idea that where Ann Kelly was, every hour of the day would be full of excitement. To Eileen, she was a comedian, as good as any you would get in a panto, she said, or on Radio Éireann.

She gave Pauline her instructions. 'Tell her we were askin' for her. Ask her to give us somethin', any little thing at all, a medal or a few sweets.'

Pauline drew her mouth into a small, tight 'o'. 'I'd be afraid to axe for anything,' she said anxiously. 'Would youse not think of sendin' her something? That would be the right thing to do. It's the visitors that's supposed to bring the presents.'

We thought for a bit about what we might have to spare, but there was another day still to go before Daddy came again, and after putting Pauline to the search, there wasn't a biscuit or a sweet to be found in any of our lockers.

'Have you not got a spare holy picture, Pauline? We could write something on the back of it.'

Pauline found the courage to say no to that. 'I'd like to oblige,' she said, 'but mine already have things writ on them, prayers and messages from them that gave them to me.'

'Well, just promise her something for when you go again,' we said, losing patience, 'and go on now, or it will be dark before you're back.'

'I don't like to go with nothin' to give.' She could be persistent when she was certain of being in the right.

'Go when you're told,' I said, 'or I'll take back that book that my daddy made me give you for your birthday.'

We watched her clumping across the line to foreign parts, moving so slowly it was plain, even to us, that she had no hope of carrying out her orders without getting caught.

And we were right about that. In less than half an hour, she was carried back like a stick doll in the arms of Sister de Montford, who raged at our nurses for letting the child go wandering off. She had never known such a thing to happen before, she said, and she would complain to Sister Finbar.

'What possessed you?' The nurses turned their rage on Pauline when the nun had gone, but Pauline was in such a state of shock she could not find words to give an account of herself, and it was a couple of days before we were able to get the full, terrible story out of her.

Pauline set out on her travels with a fluttering heart and a prayer on her lips. Her walking was improving all the time, and on a good day she was able to move quite fast and feel proud of herself. She had every hope that one of these days her prayers would be answered and she would, all of a sudden, throw off her splints to walk and skip like ordinary people, maybe even do a bit of dancing.

But this errand that had been forced on her had no pleasure in it. It was a sin of disobedience, and she had no doubt that there would be trouble at the end of it. She had hardly left the safety of her own veranda when she felt herself weighed down by nervousness and the strangeness of new ground under her feet. Here, there were no resting places, no nurses of her own to watch out for her in case she should fall over or her nerves get the better of her. She was to keep herself small, her friends had said, and not draw attention to herself.

Was it her imagination or had her head also become like a ton weight? It seemed to be pulling all the time to one side and she had no control over it. That was something new. She had always been thankful to the Lord for keeping her afflictions below the neck, for the good head and brain he had given her, but now she could hardly look from left to right without straining her whole trunk against the thick leather of her corset.

The noises around her seemed sharper, movements faster. She felt the eyes of her two friends burning holes in her back and heard their voices inside her head: 'Go on, Pauline, yer too slow. Will ya get a move on.'

At last she arrived at Ann Kelly's bed. You couldn't miss her, even without her noisiness. She was a big girl all right. She had only one splint, on her right leg, and was able to sit up and take notice of everything that went on around her. That was how she managed to be first with any news. Looking at her from a distance, you might think that she was one of the lucky ones, until you looked into her face and saw, under a fringe of blue-black hair, that her face was unnaturally fat, as if her mouth was crammed with gobstoppers. On one cheek she had a newly burst abscess, and even though it was covered, you could still see the purple edges of it, rising up from under the gauze pad and the criss-cross of sticking plaster that had one eye pushed nearly closed.

Pauline's heart turned over with a mixture of fear and pity for Ann Kelly's ugliness and the terrible thought that the poor creature must have had aspirations into her face. Forgetting her own troubles for a moment, Pauline peered through the top bars of the bed, a look of horror on her face. 'God love you,' she said, 'that wound must be terrible painful!'

Ann Kelly jerked around with a start to face her, her large, loose mouth agape. Then she said, in a voice that would terrify a saint, 'What's yer name, young one, and what in the name o' God are ye doin' up here?'

'My name is Pauline and I mean ye no harm.' Pauline released one hand from the bars and with a finger that would not be still, pointed back the way she had come. 'Them two down there were axin' for ye.'

Ann Kelly looked down towards Blessed Imelda's. 'I suppose ye mean them two eejits that are wavin' their arms.'

Pauline nodded, then winced as a stab of pain went through her neck. 'One is Eileen, the other is Rosemary.' It was a kind of relief to get the names out, as though they would now have to share in any blame that was to come. 'They said would ye give them something – please?'

'Huh! The cheek of them! I've nothin' to spare for youse brats. The best yez'll get from me is a right good thump for yerselves.'

'Ah, don't be shouting at her,' a freckled girl spoke from the next bed. 'I think Pauline is a grand little one, and isn't she marvellous, all the same, the way she has walked all the way up here to see us! You're very welcome, Pauline.'

The freckled girl lay on her back with one leg raised up on a weight and pulley. She was knitting from a big ball of blue wool, and Pauline thought her the nicest person she had ever met, with her warm smile and the welcome in her voice.

'My name is Mary,' she said. 'Now isn't that the best name of all?'

'Oh, indeed, indeed,' said Pauline.

Ann Kelly having now lost interest in her, Pauline sidled across to stand by Mary's bed. She was filled with feelings of pleasure as she watched her calmly knitting, not even having to look at the stitches but all the time smiling into Pauline's face in a kindly way, like a good mother would, and she sitting by her open door in the sunshine, with a friendly word to say to every passing stranger.

'I wish I could knit,' Pauline said.

'Sure it's easy. I'll teach you . . .' Mary began, but then seeing Pauline's bunched up fingers, 'or maybe I could knit something for you, as a present. Have you a doll at all?'

'I have, a small one. But I'm sure I could learn to make things myself if I had you to teach me.'

'OK so,' said Mary, 'we'll have a go. I'll pick out a nice colour of wool for you when the basket comes around, and I'll have it ready with the needles, the next time you come. Then, if you can't manage the knitting, sure there's plenty of other things to do. Maybe you'd like to walk right up to the end of the veranda, as far as the glass wall. There's a grand view; you could nearly see as far as the city.

'Oh, that's what they told me to do, but I'd never get that far.'

'Of course you would! You can do anything in this world, if you put you mind to it and say your prayers.'

Pauline's face took on a new radiance. The adventure suddenly became her own instead of someone else's errand. She would be able to tell her friends about the grand patients she had met on the Little Flower veranda and the wonderful things they were able to do. But that was for later. For the moment, she put out of her mind all thoughts of the two down below, who could no longer see her because she was hidden between two beds and she had no intention of looking back that way for yet awhile.

Pauline fingered the blue knitting, with its even lines of plain and purl, then, gaining courage, she gently stroked the arm of the beautiful Biddy, whose name suited her to perfection. 'I'd like to see the city, all right,' she said, 'but I'd sooner stay here with you.'

Suddenly, the scene seemed to shatter and turn upside down. Mary stopped smiling and cried out in a strangled voice, 'Oh no, please God, no!' Then she went stiff all over, her eyes disappeared up into her head and a gargling sound came from her throat. The knitting flew through the air and landed far away on the floor. Pauline looked after it miserably, so far out of reach. Mary's body began to twitch and leap all over the bed, so violently that the castors were dislodged, the bed jerked forward until one leg slipped over the edge of the veranda and embedded itself in the grass verge. Mary was tipped on to the hard ground and all her bedclothes on top of her. The bag of beans that weighted her leg swung dangerously to and fro from its pole, narrowly missing Mary's head as she lay under the avalanche of bedding, and she went on

148

jerking and jumping, with her arms flailing and white foam suds around her mouth.

Pauline, who had only just managed to step back in time to save herself from going down with the rest, clung desperately to Ann Kelly's bedclothes and buried her head in the counterpane. She was paralysed with fright, so much so that not a single prayer came into her head. All she could think of was the terrible punishment that had come upon her for going astray, and all she could hear was Ann Kelly's hoarse voice filling the air.

'Quick! Nurse! Run! Mary's havin' another fit.' There was not much urgency about her. She was just her usual, noisy self, doing what she did best – spreading the latest news. 'Hurree . . . hurree . . . Mary's on the floo-er.'

Sister de Montford came running with a nurse, and they worked at top speed to put everything to rights. Another nurse was called, and while the bed was restored to its proper place, Sister de Montford held the rigid form of Mary in her arms, then laying her gently on her mattress, she forced a steel spatula between her tightly clamped teeth to prevent her from swallowing her tongue. After a while, Mary grew still and sank into a deep sleep, but her face was moist and deathly white, her beauty distorted by the ferocity of the seizure. One of the nurses stayed close by her, with a hand on her back, watching until the crisis was well over and to make sure she had done herself no physical damage.

While all that was going on, no one saw Pauline, clinging like a tick on a sheep to the next bed, but when the worst of the crisis was over, the nun took a step backwards and almost tripped over Pauline's feet.

'Heavens, child! What on earth are you doing there?' she said, as though having suddenly discovered the cause of the trouble. 'Don't you know you're not supposed to be up here. Who gave you permission? Do you not think we have enough to do with our own patients without having to put up with unexpected visitors?'

Then, seeing how Pauline was trembling and quite unable to speak, she bent down and scooped her up into her arms. 'Don't be fretting now,' she said softly, 'it's not your fault at all. Mary is better already. Look at her now, she's fast asleep, and when she wakes up she'll be as right as rain. Will we say a little prayer for her, yes? Hail Mary, full of grace, the Lord is with thee . . .'

As Sister de Montford carried her away from the scene of devastation, Pauline's hands crept slowly up under her veil and clung to her neck. She was comforted by the words of Our Lady's prayer, the cool pressure of the nun's silver crucifix against her cheek and the warm, clean smell of starched linen. '. . . Pray for us sinners, now and at the hour of our death,' she whispered, adding inside her head, 'and thanks be to God that I haven't to walk all the way home on my own.'

Ann Kelly cupped her hands around her big, loose mouth and roared, 'Get back outa that, to yer own veranda!'

# PUNISHMENT

PAULINE'S RETURN IN the arms of Sister de Montford gave us a terrible fright. It was seldom enough that we got a close look at that nun, and even though she was cradling Pauline like a baby in her arms and calming her down with comforting words, her tone to our nurses was sharper, and they answered her with the nervous respect that her presence always commanded. 'We have nothing against a child coming up for a visit,' she said when she had finished giving out, 'but we must be told. Someone must supervise. We cannot have patients wandering all over the place . . . that is a neglect of your duty.'

The nurses, guessing that Eileen and I were behind the plan, pointed fingers and said they only hoped we realised it was a terrible thing we had done, to lead Pauline astray and she such a good little girl who never gave them any trouble. If they found out that we had anything to do with it, they said, they would separate our beds to protect Pauline from our bad example. We recognised the emptiness of their words and were not afraid of them, for we knew that they, as much as ourselves, would be anxious to keep the story from reaching the ears of the Bar. Everything must look as normal as possible by the time she came on duty.

All the while, Pauline said nothing. As soon as she was

scooped out of her harness, she lay back in her bed and, closing her eyes, continued her prayers of gratitude to be safely back in her bed. We, too, kept quiet, with looks of innocence and surprise on our faces. To think that Pauline, of all people, should take it into her head to wander off in the wrong direction! What was she thinking of at all?

By the time Pauline was able to tell us the full story, we had recovered from our fear of discovery. There had been no complaint that we knew of from Sister de Montford, and we were ready to make light of Pauline's bad experience. 'Didn't you make a new friend up there?' we said, but that only brought tears to her eyes. We called her a 'cowardy custard' and were on for making her go again and do the job properly.

'Sure, it wasn't your fault that Mary had a fit,' we argued, 'and you heard Sister de Montford say you'd be welcome to go again, as long as you ask permission.'

Our real interest lay, of course, not in poor Mary but in bringing ourselves to the notice of all the other big Biddies, especially Ann Kelly. Next time, Eileen declared, we would send a better message, write a letter maybe and send it up with a small present. But although the thought of never seeing Mary again put Pauline into a kind of mourning that had her telling her rosary beads several times a day, she refused even to talk about a future plan, and neither bribe nor threat could persuade her to go up the veranda again or even look in its direction.

Accepting at last that Pauline's stubbornness could not this time be broken, we stopped speaking to her altogether, and after Daddy's next visit she got nothing.

Pauline took her daily walk as before, down to the babies' ward where she was made welcome and praised by the nurse in charge for having got so far. A chair was put out for her, she was given a drink of milk, and after a short rest she moved from cot to cot, shaking rattles, squeaking soft toys, dangling her medals in front of the eyes of the babies, who laughed, then cried out in protest when it was time for her to leave.

'You're a great help to us, Pauline,' the nurse said. 'Won't you come again tomorrow?'

It was a long way back to her own bed, and she thought of it longingly, even though she was in no hurry to get back to her punishers. Her head leaned ever more to one side, and she could see Nurse McGinty watching her from afar with special interest.

'Now then, Pauline,' she called out. 'Hold your head up, like a good girl, and look me straight in the eye or we'll have to put the collar on you.'

Sister Finbar, who was called on for a second opinion, also looked serious and murmured secret words to the nurse. 'Walk towards us, Pauline, that's the girl. Can you straighten up your head?' The Bar's smile was encouraging and she held out her arms in a motherly way. Pauline's only wish at that moment was to please her, but her head lolled to the side and trembled of its own accord. When she tried to correct it, pain shot through her neck and down into her collarbones.

'All right, child,' the Bar said soothingly, 'get into your bed now and we'll see what doctor has to say when he comes tomorrow.'

The next day, Mr Macauley gave a lecture round Pauline's bed. Guessing that matters were serious, we felt sorry for her and began to speak to her again. It seemed certain that she would get the collar. The word travelled along the beds, 'Pauline's gettin' the collar.' 'Ah, no, not the collar.' No one told us so, but we somehow knew it had been decided, for weren't we nearly as good as doctors when it came to noticing when a patient was getting worse, instead of better!

In the evening, even though we guessed it was too late to stop it happening, the three of us said a rosary together that Pauline's head would soon stop nodding, except for when she wanted it to.

The collar was made of rigid, tan-coloured leather. About six inches high, it had soft, suede edging at the top and bottom, to keep it from chafing the skin. It was laced up the front like a workman's boot. Nurse McGinty hummed a little tune as she settled it around Pauline's neck. 'It won't be for long,' she promised. 'Don't be crying now. You'll see, it will help you.' She set Pauline on her feet and pulled out strands of her hair from under it. 'Just a little walk to begin with. See how you get on. I'll be waiting for you here.'

Pauline moved unsteadily forward. Her small white face was pushed upwards and she was hardly able to see where she was putting her feet.

'She looks like an ass lookin' over a stable door,' Eileen said behind her hand. I was thinking about singing 'Horsey, horsey, don't you stop,' to get Pauline going, but after only a few steps, she faltered and froze to the spot. Nurse McGinty rushed to help her, and as she was gently turned around, her face, tiny above the collar, was running with tears. 'I can't,' she sobbed, 'I just can't. If I was to be struck down dead, I couldn't!'

At that, we fell silent and pressed our hands over our mouths, for we, too, were having trouble in holding back the tears.

'You did very well,' said the Bar when Pauline was safely back in bed. 'Tomorrow it will be a bit easier.'

'It's the shame of it, you see,' Pauline said later, as she sat propped up in bed, curling her tongue along the edge of a custard cream. 'It's no matter if I'm made wear it for my own good. The wearing of the collar is nothing more than a disgrace and a punishment for the bad things I done.'

# THE BEGINNING OF THE END

I HAD BEEN in Cappagh for more than two years by the time my prayers were answered. 'Quite right, Sister Finbar, the leg is clean,' Mr Macauley announced one day, 'and I see no sign of another abscess.'

I watched his screwed-up face as he probed his fingers into my joints and gently pressed down on my thigh, and was so surprised by his next words that I felt no immediate excitement. 'I think we could have her off the frame for a wee while in the afternoons,' he said, as if it was quite an ordinary kind of decision. 'What do you think, Sister?'

The Bar nodded her head vigorously, and her smile was so wide that her headgear gaped at the sides and I could see two tufts of grey hair falling straight down in front of her ears. 'We'll send her down to the gym, to get the legs moving,' she said.

Did I really hear that, or was it only my imagination?

'Is it true?' I asked the Bar when she came back, still smiling.

'Of course, it is. Didn't I tell you all along the day would come? I will telephone your daddy as soon as I have a minute and give him the news.'

I told Mummy at once, covering my eyes and calling her to listen, even though it was early in the day and I knew she would be up to her eyes looking after

Stephanie. This was urgent, I told her, and she came at once into my head. She was standing in the middle of the hall at home in the velvet housecoat, her hand over her heart and the tears pouring down her face. When she spoke, her voice was all shaky.'Oh darling, I can't believe it. It's just too marvellous for words!'

'Don't cry, Mummy,' I comforted her. 'You won't feel the time going till I'll be home to help you with the baby.'

The nurses were in great good humour as they unbuckled all my straps. They said it was a good feeling for them as well, to be releasing patients instead of always having to tie them down.

'How long have you been here now?' they asked.

'Two years and three months,' I told them.

'Long enough. Sure you'll soon be leaving us, and what will we do without you at all?'

'I'll come back to visit,' I promised, 'and I'll probably bring my little sister.'

'We'll look forward to that,' they said.

One of them lifted me up clear of the bed, saying I was as light as a feather out of my frame. The other nurse pulled the frame out from under me and stood it on the floor, resting it against the bedhead. I looked with shame and disgust at the padded saddle on which I had lain for so long. It was worn bare in places, nearly through to the horsehair stuffing. The waterproof cover was stained and discoloured and had a bad smell. It stood there for all to see, like a corpse without a head.

'Phew!' said the nurse. We'll have to find you a fresh one of those.'

'Why would you bother?' I pleaded. 'Sure I won't be needing it for much longer.'

I tensed myself against the pain as they cut through

the thick layers of strapping and peeled it away from my legs, replacing it with fresh plaster and bandage, but so much lighter than before, just enough to anchor me down at night. They changed me into a sitting-up gown, with a seam down the back instead of tapes, then carefully turned me over to lie on my front. There was neither iron nor leather to keep me away from the cool smoothness of the sheets. When they had pulled up my covers and tucked me in, I raised my head like a tortoise coming out of its shell and slowly looked around me. 'Your face looks different from up here,' I told Eileen.

'If 'ou could only see 'ourself!' she laughed, 'with 'our hair sticking up like a sweeping brush!'

The nurse worked at it with a heavy hand and a wet hairbrush but it was hopeless. The long straight hair I once had now grew upwards and would not lie down. 'Give it time,' she said. 'Rome wasn't built in a day.'

They left me alone to get used to my new position, and I felt as proud as if I had won a prize, but soon a mist came suddenly over my sight and everything began to rush past in a screaming gale, faster and faster. Trees, beds, curiously staring faces, all merged into a huge, humming top. There was a pounding in my ears as I was sucked into the middle of it and there was nothing – no one – to hold on to.

'Holy Mammy, save me,' I tried to shout. 'I'm going blind.'

But no one answered.

I opened my eyes to find myself back in the afternoon peace of the veranda, with life going on as if nothing extraordinary had happened. My cheek was resting comfortably on a small, flat pillow and a nurse was gently patting my back.

'Just a little dizzy spell,' she said, holding a beaker of

water to my lips. 'That's quite normal when you've been lying so long on your back.'

My bare, stripped legs were raw, like a pair of skinned rabbits and nearly as helpless. It was as much as I could do to raise even the good one an inch off the mattress. I reached down to touch the flaky skin that had for so long been hidden from view. I stroked it and gently scratched the bits that I was able to reach, until the flesh tingled and burned and patches of dead skin loosened around the edges. As my nails drew blood, a fit of fear took hold of me and I realised the damage I might do. For all the progress they said my leg was making, the best I had to show after all this time was a weak and useless stick of a thing that would never be the match of the good one. It looked as if it might snap like a stick of barley sugar as soon as weight was put on it.

Nurse McGinty painted my raw thigh with bright red mercurochrome. 'There's to be no scratching,' she roared, 'or you will go septic!'

'Exercise is what you need now.' Sister Finbar held up a clenched fist. 'Your calves must be this hard and you will have to be able to kick your buttocks with your heels before we can let you put your feet on the floor.'

I tried to take heart from her words, but my elation had all but melted away as I contemplated the enormity of the task that lay ahead of me. What if I could not do it? I had no faith in that sore, skinny leg, and thought it quite likely that I would have to spend the rest of my life in bed.

One night I dreamed of Kathleen O'Donnell. She was creeping across the cold floor of the veranda on all fours and singing,

> *Oh the days of the Kerry dancing,*
> *Oh the ring of the piper's tune . . .*

Waking, I wondered why it was that she had not seemed to care that she would never, in this life anyway, stand upright on the floor – let alone dance to the tune of a piper – but was content with her lot because it brought her attention and petting that she would never have got without her hump. I never asked the question out loud, for I already knew the answer; it was because she had resigned herself to God's will, and that was the only way to be certain of gaining a good place in heaven.

But more than heaven, I wanted to go home to Sandycove, to be with my family, wear a school uniform and be chosen to join in the team games.

> *Stands the lady on the mountain, who she is I do not know.*
> *All she wants is gold and silver, into the circle you will go.*

Another dream that I had more than once during that time was of flying in the sky, like the bird Daddy had bought one time at the Sunday morning bird market in Dublin.

'A linnet, sir,' the man had said. 'She will gladden your heart with song.' But we waited in vain for the bird to sing. All it did was beat its wings against the bars with increasing frenzy.

'It's terrified,' Mummy said. 'It'll beat itself to death.' So Daddy carried the cage into the garden and unlatched the door. At first the bird did not realise it was being offered its freedom but continued to beat and flap its wings until Daddy reached in with a gloved hand and lifted it out. Then he released it into the sky and it soared upwards and was soon lost to our sight.

Did it ever find its way home? I often wondered.

Physiotherapy days were so cheerful that I soon began to feel more hopeful. As I was wheeled down the veranda, I held my head high and, with all the airs and graces of a senior Biddy, smiled and said, 'Hello and how are you?' to the little ones, who watched my passing with the same kind of respect that we, in our turn, felt for the Little Flowers.

Down past the babies' ward we went, over the noisy ramp towards the green-tiled corridor that led to the operating theatre, but turning aside, without fear, towards the double doors of the gymnasium.

The big, square hall was festooned with ropes and climbing frames, dumb-bells stacked on shelves along the wall. The beds were lined up in the middle.

'One, two! One, two!' Miss Nolan leapt about to the sound of marching music on a wind-up gramophone, grabbing hold of a leg here, an arm there, turning heads this way and that between her spotlessly clean hands. 'Come on now, kick out! Draw big circles with those arms – pretend you're painting a ceiling! Heads up! Arms up! Let's see those heels! Up! Up! Up!'

It did you no good to be downhearted in Miss Nolan's presence. She just would not allow it.

As the weeks passed, Johnnies and Biddies of all shapes and sizes got over their shyness and, with the urging on of Miss Nolan and a good measure of divine assistance, began to achieve the impossible.

'*My darling,*' Mummy wrote,

> *What a joy to hear that you are off your frame. I still think of you all the time, and as soon as you are ready to come home, I will buy you a trousseau fit for a bride.*

I showed my letter to the night nurses, as they warmed their hands in their armpits.

'A trousseau indeed! Oh, you're very posh altogether.'

'Just what I need, a trousseau.'

'You'll need to find a man first – and a rich one at that.'

I laughed at their teasing and felt sorry for them, for I knew they were not rich and had to work very hard for a living. They could not afford to go shopping in Grafton Street, buying only the best of everything the way Mummy did.

As my heels got closer – and closer – to my buttocks, happier dreams of being at home returned, and I saw myself in shoes and socks, taking my sister for long walks in her pram and skipping with playmates in a school playground.

# CHANGES

LTHOUGH OUR TENTH birthdays were still a long way off, the subject of our move to the Little Flower's ward was more often discussed. It had more to do with our schooling than our treatment, Wastras said, but more important still was the big news that the Archbishop of Dublin was coming to confirm in the faith all those who were considered ready and worthy of the sacrament.

'You know, he only comes once in three years to every parish,' she said to Sister Finbar, 'so even though these three girls are on the young side, they'll need to catch him this time around and get moved up for Sister Patrick's instruction classes.'

Sister Finbar agreed. It shocked us that she showed no sadness at the thought of losing us.

'Will you not be sorry?' I asked.

She gave her usual chuckle, as if I had said something amusing. 'Of course, I will, but we have patients waiting for beds. You three are growing up fast and are well on the mend now.'

'I thought I was your pet,' I reproached her.

'No, I am,' Eileen insisted.

'You are all my pets,' she said, handing out biscuits from a paper bag that she had lifted from somebody's locker, 'and sure, you'll be no more than a few yards away. You're not going to the moon.'

No date was set for our move, but I felt I had already lost her. Knowing so well her daily habits and how busy she always was, I knew that once out from under her eye, she would be giving all her attention to her new patients and would scarcely have time even to give me a wave.

'I'll be sad to leave you,' Pauline said, 'though Sister de Montford is nice, mind you.'

'Well, you, Pauline, won't be staying with us for much longer.' Sister Finbar picked up Pauline's hand and rubbed it between her own, as though to polish away the stiffness. 'As soon as you have made your confirmation, you'll be going to the convalescent home.'

Pauline's eyes looked suddenly enormous, and if it was possible for her to go paler than she already was, this was the moment.

'Why would I be going there? Wouldn't I be a stranger!' She clutched on to Sister Finbar's hand as though she expected at any moment to be wrenched away from her. 'Please, don't think of sending me away, Sister.'

'Ah now, don't fret – you will love it there,' the Bar explained, 'Everyone will be up and about, so there will be great activity and games. You will soon settle and make new friends.'

'Will I be staying there for ever?'

'Well, maybe not for ever but a good long time anyway. And you wouldn't want to stay here for ever now, would you?'

We went quiet after she left us, thinking in our different ways about the future. Even Eileen looked solemn for a few minutes, now that the time had come.

I knew only one thing for sure – that Sister de Montford, for all her kindness, would never take the place of Sister Finbar in my heart. You only had to see the two of them, kneeling side by side on the floor at the holiest part of the mass, to know they were as different as chalk to cheese. Sister Finbar was as rosy and comforting to behold as the other nun was pale and serious. There was no doubt about which one of them I would choose to be with, and I imagined that even Daddy would have his work cut out to raise a bit of a laugh out of Sister de Montford.

But we soon put our worries to the backs of our minds and talked instead, as we had so often done before the plans were announced, about the joys of becoming big Biddies. Eileen saw it all as a great improvement and said she would never look back once she had found her place on the Little Flower veranda. For me, there would also be the great relief of getting away from Wastras. I seemed to be always annoying her and was still smarting from the row over little Una's knitting, which had fallen on the floor and some nurse, in a hurry to tidy up, had picked it up and stuffed it into my locker. It was missing for days. Little Una cried and said the girls must have swept it away or else someone had stolen it. Then Wastras, as though guided by divine inspiration, opened my locker one morning, and there it was, in a tangled heap, with most of its stitches dropped. No words were spoken as she slowly took it out and dangled it in front of my eyes, but the look on her face accused me of grievous sin, and I knew, even as I protested my innocence, that she did not want to believe me. I watched the senior teacher every day for any warning signs of nastiness but saw none. I warmed to her pleasant smile and the way she moved calmly from bed to bed, enjoying herself with her pupils. Her only fault, as far as I could see, was that she was not much of a singer.

'Still gawking up the veranda,' Wastras pounced on me morning. Her voice was hoarse with shouting out the lesson, of which I had not heard a single word. 'I think you should go up there today. Some will be glad to see the back of you. Now, will you answer the question?'

'Is it the Glory Be we're supposed to be sayin'?'

She slapped her book down on my chest and her voice rose to a squeak. 'Am I wasting my time here, or what? The question is, what do you call the archbishop, if he is foolish enough to speak to you?'

Oh the relief! She would have to give me a word of praise now, for I knew the answer.

Paul had made his confirmation long ago, and I remembered all the words that went with the occasion. 'Your Grace,' I said, smiling up at her.

'Huh! A lucky guess,' was all she said before going on her way.

# SOLDIERS OF CHRIST

'CONFIRMATION,' SAID SISTER Patrick, 'is a truly wonderful sacrament. When you are confirmed, the Holy Ghost comes down upon you and you become a strong and perfect Christian – a soldier of Christ, ready to defend Him every day of your life and if necessary to die for Him.'

We were not moved on after all, thanks, in the end, to Sister de Montford who put forward several objections. She said it would be a month at least before she could see her way to accepting us on her ward, and anyway, where was the sense in unsettling us when we would probably all be gone out of the hospital by the end of the year. Those were the first words we had heard about going home. We received them with delight and felt much better about Sister de Montford from that day on.

So for a time, we had the best of both worlds, being the most senior patients on our own veranda, which was better, we agreed, than being new girls in an unfamiliar place. Twice a week we were wheeled importantly over the dividing line into a quiet area of the Little Flower's ward to attend the special confirmation classes. Alongside the big Biddies, we chanted with the best of them the answers to questions out of the long green catechism, even though there were still parts of the small, pink one that we were by no means sure of. Over and over, Sister Patrick had us repeating the words we had to learn, so that we would never forget them and could nearly say them in our sleep. At the end of each lesson we were wheeled back to our own places, which, in our tiredness, gave us the comforting sense of going home.

Wastras held discussions with Sister Patrick about how young we were and whether we could be made ready in the short time available, bearing in mind that His Grace might hop on any one of us and ask a question which we would be expected to answer without hesitation. 'Wouldn't it reflect badly on the teaching so far,' she said anxiously, 'and on the children themselves, if they were to fail the test?'

Sister Patrick patted the teacher's arm in her kindly way and told her to put her mind at rest. 'They are a special case,' she said, 'and I will make sure that His Grace is made aware of the situation. As long as they have a good understanding of what it means to be confirmed, allowances will be made.'

We were delighted to see Sister Patrick again, to have her full attention for six whole weeks. It seemed a long time to us, since she had prepared us for our first Holy Communion.

'We remember you well,' we told her, thinking she would be pleased, but she answered us with a frown, as if we had said something wrong.

'Of course, you do! No matter how long you live and wherever you go throughout your lives, you will never forget the person who first taught you about the love of Jesus and made you ready to receive His sanctifying grace in the blessed sacrament.'

But we were never really shamed by her, she was so full of charity and good humour. We looked forward to the days of her lessons, listening for the bus just we did on visiting days.

'Now, it's all very well for you Catholic children,' she told us, 'living as you do in the South of Ireland, where there is no persecution, thank God. But say you lived in Belfast, now . . . That is not so very far away – you don't have to go to Africa to find heathens, you know. In Belfast, Protestants parade around the streets, singing dreadful songs that are an insult to Our Lady and our Holy Father, the pope. What about that now? Would you have the courage to stand up and profess your faith in the light of that?'

'Of course, we would,' said Pauline, as strongly as she was able. 'I would rather die a martyr's death than deny my Saviour.'

Sister Patrick raised a warning finger. 'You could be sorely tested. Remember poor Saint Peter?' And she told again how, after Jesus had been arrested, Saint Peter was standing around the fire with a crowd of people, warming his hands, and when one of them thought they recognised him, he was afraid to admit that he was one of the apostles. 'Not once did he betray his best friend, not twice, but three times! "I know not the man," were the words he said.'

'I could never do such a terrible thing,' I said. 'That was the worst sin that was ever committed. I can't understand why Saint Peter was ever forgiven.'

'Jesus loves the repentant sinner,' Sister Patrick said simply.

You would think, listening to her, that it was a good idea to go off and commit sins for a while, just so that Jesus would be delighted when you came back and said you were sorry.

'But we all say hurtful things sometimes, don't we? And don't find it easy to accuse ourselves.'

'If I ever heard anyone sayin' a word against Jesus,'

Eileen said, 'or for that matter, Our Lady, God, I'd crucify them!'

At that, the big Biddies roared with laughing and
Eileen, for once embarrassed, clapped her hand over her
mouth.

'We won't be asking you to crucify anyone at all,' said
Sister Patrick cheerfully, ' but it's good to know that the
Lord can depend on you three at least to defend His
name – and never forget, any of you, that He is always
there beside you. He sees all, He knows all.'

# Paul's Big Day

I WAS OFTEN reminded during that time of the day Paul made his confirmation at the Pro-Cathedral. Pupils from schools all over the city were gathered in for the ceremony, and there were so many of them that there was no room inside the church for any of their relations. They all had to be in their places by half past eight in the morning and sit quietly saying their prayers until the archbishop arrived at ten o'clock.

After leaving Paul at the door, Mummy and I spent the morning in Grafton Street, strolling through the big shops, looking at all the lovely clothes and shoes. Mummy bought herself a pure silk scarf, a yellow one. She said yellow was her favourite colour because it reminded her of sunshine. After coffee in Mitchell's, we went to collect Daddy from his office, and the three of us walked together across O'Connell Bridge, holding hands. I had no sign of a bad leg then and was able to jump and run between them as they stepped out, hurrying to get out of the strong breeze that was blowing up the Liffey from the sea.

We reached the Pro-Cathedral at the arranged time of one o'clock, but there was no sign of anyone coming out. It was cold waiting on the steps, listening to the powerful sound of thousands of raised voices singing:

*Great Paraclete to thee we cry*
*Oh highest gift of God most high.*

171

At that time I did not know the meaning of the word 'Paraclete', and Daddy explained that it was just another name for the Holy Ghost.

Mummy was shivering inside her musquash coat and looking disagreeable, as if it was all Daddy's fault that she had to be there at all, in a run-down part of the city where she wouldn't normally be seen dead. Daddy was in bad humour as well. He paced up and down, glaring through the doors of the church at the backs of the congregation that filled the doorway. 'Come on out of that,' he kept saying. 'Don't make a meal of it!'

It was not far short of two o'clock when the crowds began to emerge. First came the orphan boys, two by two in their strange uniforms, their boots striking the ground like a rain of hammer blows. They were followed by the girl orphans and poor children from the National Schools, all togged out in frilly white dresses and veils for the occasion. Some of the boys were dressed in little men's suits, which Mummy said was a terrible way to dress a child. Others were only able to manage clean, but-toned-up jumpers and had their hair wetted back off their scrubbed faces. Last to come out were the boys and girls from the colleges and convents. They had been sitting in the front pews, and each school was recognisable by its own special uniform. The girls wore white gloves and walked at an even, dignified pace.

I ran forward when I spotted the Belvedere boys, standing out impressively in their black and white braid-ed blazers and first long trousers, searching for Paul. With Daddy's encouragement, I was planning to greet him with a 'Hello, Charlie!' for that was the name he had taken as a confirmed Christian. But when at last he appeared, he swept past me like a blind man and made a beeline for Mummy where she stood tucked in out of the draught behind a stone pillar, and the minute he reached her, he burst into tears.

'Come on, old man,' Daddy said to jolly up the party, 'we'll have a slap-up lunch. As a special treat, I'll take you to Stickfoot's, where the chef stirs the soup with his wooden leg and the mugs are all chained to the tables.' I laughed although I had heard the joke many times before, but Paul shrugged away from him and Mummy was still annoyed.

'Leave him alone,' she said to Daddy. 'Can't you see he has had a terrible morning in that stuffy old church. I'm surprised he didn't faint!'

We went to the Grill Room at the Dolphin Hotel – the best restaurant in town, Daddy said. The raw meat was laid out in a glass cabinet for you to examine and then choose the piece you fancied. Then the chef, in a tall white hat, picked it up on the prongs of a long fork and tossed it under a red-hot grill to cook exactly to your taste. I asked for a pork chop, but when it arrived it was burnt on the outside and pink in the middle. Daddy called the waiter with a sweep of his arm and complained so charmingly that no one got cross. The chop was taken away and I got chicken instead, followed by two puddings, which we didn't have to pay for.

As we ate, Paul told us feelingly about the ordeal he had been through, with hundreds of bodies packed closely into the pews shoulder to shoulder, and while his feet got colder and colder, his upper half burned in the suffocating fug of all the open mouths, singing and breathing the stale air in and out again. When it was the turn of his pew to go up to the altar, it had taken nearly half an hour of shuffling, an inch at a time, to reach the throne on which the archbishop sat. 'He leaned forward,' Paul said, getting carried away, 'anointed my forehead with chrism and then slapped me ruthlessly across the face.'

'Now, then,' Daddy said, 'let's have less of the superlatives. That poor old boy hasn't the strength to pull the skin off a rice pudding.'

I could still feel sorry that Paul's big day had been more of a penance than a pleasure, and I was very thankful that ours was a different archbishop, who was taking the trouble to come out to Cappagh since, of course, we were not able to travel up to the Pro-Cathedral. For us, there would be no hanging around in the cold for everyone to get worn out and bad-tempered. We would not, of course, be celebrating the occasion in a smart Grill Room, but for us, God's special children, it was going to be a day of spiritual gifts and blessings, which, as Sister Patrick said, we would remember with joy for the rest of our lives.

But wasn't it a pity all the same, I thought to myself, that Paul's first action as a strong and perfect Christian was to show a child's weakness?

# Boots and Shoes

VERY DAY WE watched Pauline, moving now at a rate of knots along the veranda, anxious always to get down to the safety of the babies' ward. Leather squeaking, boots clumping, she would remind you of a wooden puppet, jerkily guided along by invisible strings. She could go the whole distance now without having to stop for a rest and had even grown used to wearing the collar, which she now saw as a test of her faith and no punishment at all.

'I'm getting' better all the time, amn't I?' She demanded her daily praise, and there was a fondness in Sister Finbar's eyes as she gave it and, little by little, prepared Pauline for her move to the convalescent home.

For me, there seemed to be no movement at all. Mr Macauley passed me by with barely a nod, and home was never mentioned, except in Mummy's letters. We would have great times, she always promised, but those images of perfect happiness were for the moment secondary to the importance of getting my feet on the floor. The last thing I wanted was to leave here, like Kathleen O'Donnell, in a wheelchair.

Every day was the same as the one before. I was taken off my frame in the afternoon, turned over on my front and told to 'keep aiming for those buttocks'. I did everything I was told, but although the good leg quickly returned to normal bending, the joint of the right knee remained stiff and the hip completely immovable, as if there had never been a joint there at all.

'Only that far to go.' Miss Nolan held up her two fore-fingers only inches apart, but there might as well have been a mile-wide gap between them.

Little Una had more go in her these days and had begun to speak up for herself. 'Aren't you very blessed all the same,' she said in a kind of huff, ' bein' off your frame every day.You should be thankin' God for his good-ness to you. I've no idea when I'll be getting' off mine.'

'You're not on it long enough,' I told her. 'I'd say it will be another year, at the very least, before you get to my stage.'

Una's mouth went down at the corners, but she nod-ded her head, accepting this as the probable truth.

'It's different for everyone.' Pauline poked her face through the bars of Una's bedhead. 'A patient could be sittin' up three months after comin' in, on the floor in six months and home again in a year. You never know. It all depends on how many abscesses you get.'

Still worried, Una said, 'Well, I only hope I won't still be here with all these young ones after youse have all gone home, or up there.' She pointed towards the Little Flower veranda.

'Some of us will be gone all right,' said Pauline, 'but Rosemary will be here for yet a while. Sure she hasn't even been fitted for her boots yet.'

'Boots! What do you mean boots?' She might as well have said that my soul was damned to hell. 'Who told you I was having boots? You don't know anything.'

'Everyone has to have boots.' Pauline moved across to my bed and with the voice of experience said, 'You might as well resign yourself and offer it up.'

'Go to hell,' I said, pushing her away. She would have fallen on the floor if she hadn't had a good hold on the bars.

The day we first saw Pauline's boots, long ago it now seemed, we had all shown great interest in them and listened with envy as she described the feel of them on her feet and around her ankles. 'They're soft, but then again strong . . . well, sensible like. They protect you, keep you standing up when your legs are too weak.'

It took her a while to get used to them, of course, and though she would never admit to the extent of her pain, great relief showed in her face when, after her walk, the boots were eased off her sore, pink feet and they were rubbed vigorously with surgical spirit to harden them up. Pauline loved her boots and was loyal to them. They belonged to her, and while they were still a novelty, she cradled them in her arms like a pair of twin babies. When she was ready to share her pleasure in them, she passed them first to me and then to Eileen for our approval. We examined them closely, smelled the leather and pushed our hands deep down inside them. They were good boots all right, and in those early days, when walking was only something to imagine, I would have agreed to wear wooden boxes on my feet if only I could be allowed to take up my bed and walk.

But it had been one of Mummy's fondest hopes, right from the start, that once I was cured of my wretched disease, I would be able to wear proper shoes. I, of course, agreed with her, for I had only ever seen boots on the feet of labouring men. At the time, we all thought I would be going home in just a few weeks, but Sister Finbar had soon put an end to our ignorance, saying it was far too early to be thinking about footwear. Then Mummy got sick and wasn't able to visit me, and soon afterwards, with the baby coming so unexpectedly, the subject was not in the front of anyone's mind but my own. I well knew Mummy's taste in fashion, she being the most elegant lady in Sandycove. Boots would never be acceptable to her, I knew, and so I would be ashamed to be seen in them.

'I'm having shoes,' I announced firmly, 'and that's that!'

'They'll be no good for 'ou,' Eileen added her gleeful voice to the discussion. 'They won't support 'our ankles and 'ou'll fall over.'

'You will get neither boots nor shoes,' said a nurse, passing by in a hurry, 'unless and until you get those heels up.'

Daddy said, 'Go on, give yourself a good kick in the backside – look, it's easy!' He performed a few jumps and contortions, but for once I could not laugh, either at that moment or maybe ever again, and the pleasurable thoughts of getting out of bed were spoiled for me by a new set of fears.

'It won't be long now,' said the Bar at the end of a bad day. 'Ask the Little Flower to help you. Haven't you a great devotion to her? Remember how patient she had to be when she longed to enter the Carmelite Order before she was old enough? She had to wait, didn't she? She prayed and petitioned the pope until he relented and allowed her to enter when she was hardly more than a child.'

I had, it was true, been praying to that saint for so long I thought she should be very fond of me by now. I knew exactly what she looked like, had seen on many a holy picture that face of a radiant nun with a lap full of roses, each one representing the answer to someone's prayer. 'Send us a rose,' we prayed. It was always the roses that brought out the piety in us.

Wastras brought in a book one day which told the whole story of the Little Flower during her life on earth. There were real photographs of the gently smiling saint. She smiled even when scrubbing the floor of the convent, and we were told she was riddled with a wasting disease and in great pain all the time. We pored over the scenes of her childhood, the faces of her family at home, and were only amazed that a saint could have lived in the time of cameras.

And yet . . . to me the story was worrying, for no sooner was Therese in the convent than she was praying for herself and her parents and sisters to die. She had what was called a beatific vision of heaven, which put her into a state of ecstasy so that she welcomed her pain and sickness as the tools that brought her closer to God.

That was all very well, but I thought it a peculiar thing that anyone should wish for death, especially a young girl who had not, by a long shot, lived out her days on earth. Wasn't it a cure that we were all yearning for? If the Little Flower cared so little about life, how could she be expected to take an interest in boots and shoes?

It would be better, I decided, to ask Saint Bernadette, who was well known for getting miracles performed on the blind, the lame and the sorely afflicted. From the shrine at Lourdes, where the saint had regular meetings with the Immaculate Conception, we were told that thousands went home cured, leaving behind their crutches, callipers and more than likely their surgical boots as well.

My first school shoes were brown, to match my uniform. In Bradley's shoe shop on Nassau Street, they X-rayed my feet and I saw the skeleton of my toes on a screen. 'Growing feet should never be cramped,' the assistant said, so Mummy bought the new shoes two sizes larger than my summer sandals. I was so pleased with them I begged to be allowed to wear them at once, even though it was raining and they might be in danger of getting spotted.

My feet felt huge and clumsy as we hurried along to Grafton Street. Mummy loved Grafton Street, where all the best shops were. I clutched the string of a blue, gas-filled balloon, which every child was given on leaving the shoe shop. It had 'Bradley's' printed on it, so everyone we passed in the street would know that I had new shoes on me and where they had been bought.

In Mitchell's teashop Mummy met her friends for tea. They talked about only ever buying clothes with good labels on them: 'None of your rubbish from the cheap shops, thank you very much.' They discussed the great time they had had at the golf club dinner, where the appearance and behaviour of some of the wives left much to be desired. I chose two cakes from the trolley, and while I was making up my mind which one to eat first, the string of the balloon came undone from the back of my chair, and it rose slowly into the air until it reached the rosette on the high yellowed ceiling. There it stayed with the string dangling down. The ladies were amused but no one tried to get it down for me. 'You couldn't possibly,' Mummy said.

Maybe it was still there, for all anyone knew – out of reach – and my shoes given to Titchy of the Buildings, along with my tricycle and the beautiful yellow cardigan that Mrs Bower had knitted for my last birthday at home.

# STANDS THE LADY ON THE MOUNTAIN

IN THE DEAD of night the field was navy blue, the altar a huge, darker shadow against the starry sky. The trees shivered and whispered the way they always did, even in the mildest of weather. Along the veranda, not a child stirred. Inside the ward, a single light shone at the desk where a night nurse sat, also quite still, her veil removed and lying on the desk in front of her, her chin resting on her chest.

I lay awake thinking that Sister Joan must have come and gone for such peace to be possible, and as always when I could not sleep, I turned my thoughts to home and Mummy. Tonight, her features would not come clear except for the tear on her cheek, but I could make out the shape of her, at one moment in her own, elegant clothes, reading out social announcements in *The Irish Times*, then fading into the paler shades of my heavenly mother, to whom I prayed for my special intentions.

'Holy Mother of God – and my mother, too – hear my prayer and let me go home out of this. My leg is nearly better. I know I still have the wounds but the doctor says they're clean. And yet, they keep me in bed while Pauline, who has neither a good leg nor a good arm on her, is up every day and will soon be discharged to the convalescent home.'

Out in the darkness, an unusual glow caught my eye. It was like a street lamp in a fog, and it hovered over the spot where the Immaculate Conception stood. The light then formed itself into a silver ring – a halo – and under it a face appeared, the face of my heavenly mother, every feature clear and dearly familiar. Her lips were moving but I could hear no words. As the mist rolled back and her body became visible, she raised her two arms as if to call me over. 'Come!' she seemed to be saying. 'Come to me!'

I looked down and saw that my arms had changed into white wings. I rose up slowly from my bed, shaking off my bonds like an ascending bird. Then I was flying like Peter Pan, with my nightdress flapping against my legs, out over the fields and carried by the wind across Dublin Bay, with its white, dancing waves and a semi-circle of diamond lights far below me.

'Which way, which way?' I cried. 'Please, can you tell me the way to Sandycove?'

'Over there, look! You can't miss it,' a kindly voice replied. Then a chorus of men's voices broke in, 'We'll give you a "Carry the Lady to London, to London, to London."'

'Oh, thank you, I can see it now. I need to get there in a hurry.'

The voices grew faint as I left them far behind and hurtled on, skimming across the dark waters, then soaring upwards into the night sky, trying to reach that one light that was brighter than all the others but which never seemed to come any closer.

I woke up with tears on my face. From the soreness of my throat and the tightness of my chest, I guessed I had been sobbing in my sleep. It was still dark but for the one light inside the ward. All my buckles were undone, my bedclothes sagging towards the floor. Sister Patrick's words came into my head: 'He made the blind to see and the lame to walk.' All those miracles were true, she had assured us and bestowed on those whose faith was strong enough. 'Faith can move mountains,' she said.

I made the sign of the cross, the way I used to see the swimmers do before diving into deep water. I began to ease myself out of my frame, pulling apart as best I could the bars across my chest. Slipping off the bedclothes I moved sideways and swung my legs gingerly over the edge of the mattress. It was a long way down to the floor, and for a moment, caught halfway, my courage almost failed me. Thoughts of terrible injury and punishment took over, and I would have given everything I owned to be back in the safety of my frame. Too late! A moment later I felt the cold ground pressing on the soles of my feet and a chill breeze around my ankles. And then – oh, the giddy feel of being upright! I could have stood there for ever, giving myself over to the tingling pleasure that took hold of me from head to toe, inside and out, and the realisation that I need no longer be a bed-patient but was strong enough to bear my own weight.

There was no going back now. A wave of determination gave me the courage to put one foot in front of the other, then the other . . . and the other . . . and the other. 'One potato, two potato, three potato four – five potato, six potato, seven potato, more!'

Ten sideways steps it took to travel across the top of the bed and then, after a pause to rest, ten steps back again, and there was no pain, no weakness in the head, no fear now, except of being caught.

The thrill died when I arrived back at my starting point and found that I could not lift myself back into the bed, which was more than waist high. My legs were tired now and freezing cold, my arms weakened by the effort of pulling myself along. I stood still for what seemed like an hour, clinging to the bedhead, calling on Our Lady to come and help me quickly, but she had vanished into the night. I was all alone and feared that at any moment I would slide down the leg of the bed to lie on the hard floor, undiscovered until morning. There was nothing for it but to call for human assistance, tell the nurse I had fallen out of bed in the middle of a bad dream, about growing wings and flying through the sky. Well, that was the truth, wasn't it? Nearly.

I decided to try Eileen first. 'Wake up!' I hissed at her. 'I'm in trouble. Eileen, wake up!'

Eileen's head appeared from under her humped-up blankets. 'Jesus, Mary and Joseph!' She blinked several times. 'Didn't I only think 'ou were Kathleen O'Donnell, comin' to haunt me again.'

'I'm stuck. I can't get back into my bed.'

With hardly a moment's hesitation, Eileen went to work on her own straps and fearlessly leaned out, so far that there was every chance the two of us would end up in a heap on the floor. That didn't seem such a bad thought. At least then the two of us would share the blame. Eileen managed to get a fistful of my mattress and pull the beds towards each other, in such a well-practised way that the castors turned sideways without a squeak and hardly a sound was made. Then she collapsed into one of her giggling fits and had to take a short rest to smother her snorts and gurgles with a blanket.

'God, this is great gas,' she said in a loud whisper. 'Now 'ou're squashed between the two beds so 'ou can't fall down.'

'It's not funny.' I was in tears now. 'My feet are freezing and I want is to be back in my bed with no sins on my soul.'

184

Eileen reached out and somehow got her two hands under my armpits, while I grasped the bars of the bed-head and tried to pull myself up. It was hard going for both of us, but not for a moment did she loosen her hold. Twice we had to pause and rest, clinging to each other, with me crying into her shoulder and she whispering encouragement into my ear. 'Come on now, 'ou're nearly there.' In the end, we managed between us to haul me back into the bed.

'Now, maybe 'ou will give me a bit of peace,' Eileen said as I struggled back into my frame. She pulled her comfort blanket over her head and within a few seconds seemed to be fast asleep.

For me it was not so easy. I lay awake for a long time, gasping over my own audacity, wondering if it was a real vision I had had or only a dream put into my head by the devil maybe, to lead me into temptation. I was just drifting off when Eileen's first words on waking came back to me.

'What did you mean, you thought I was Kathleen O'Donnell? Wake up this minute, Eileen, and tell me what you were talking about.'

Eileen's blanket moved only slightly and an eye peered out from the folds. 'That's twice 'ou woke me up,' she said. She lay unmoving for a while, then as sleep deserted her, she poked her whole head out and hissed at me with slow patience, as though explaining something simple to a halfwit. 'Did she not tell us she would come back to visit us?'

'Well, yes, but . . .'

'Them were the last words she shouted out from the anubulce.'

'Ambulance,' I corrected her.

'Anublance.'

185

'She meant really come to visit us, like on the bus – on an excursion day – not in a holy vision. Sure, she didn't know she was going to die.'

'Well, that's what she said anyway, and she has kept her promise. I seen her tree times now!'

'You're telling lies . . .' I began, but then stopped to think. How could I be sure of anything, considering all I had been through tonight. 'Maybe it's only dreams we do have,' I said.

'No dream at all. Only a vision.' Eileen thrust an arm out and licking her finger, delved into the blanket again and made a sign of the cross on her chest. 'I do see her as clear as I see 'ou now – cross my heart and hope to die. She does be wearin' a white dress, the golden roses in her hair, and she does be singin' hymns at the top of her voice.'

'Where do you see her?'

'All over the place. In the sky sometimes, or sittin' in this very bed beside me. I can feel the warumth of her.'

'Has she the hump?'

'Can't say I've noticed the hump.'

'Does she speak? What kind of things does she say?'

'All sorts. She does say she is in great form and does be prayin' for us all.'

'But why?' I was beginning to feel annoyed now. 'I can't understand why it's you that she chooses to haunt – visit.'

Eileen shrugged. 'How do I know? Maybe because I was always good to her.'

'You were not! You used always be telling her to shut up.'

'So did you.'

'Well, I used to give her things, didn't I? Shared my presents, so I did. Look at how good my daddy was to her,

186

every week. You'd think she would choose me before you.'

Eileen poked her tongue out and immediately covered her head again.

'Eileen, wait! Come here till I tell you something really true – but you must swear never to tell a living soul.'

'Will 'ou for God's sake go to sleep now.'

'I saw Our Lady tonight.'

Eileen did not stir or show any part of herself again. There was a limit to what she was prepared to put up with.

# JUST DESERTS

'GIVE US A lend of your *Dandy*.'

'Later.'

'No, now!'

Meek as a lamb I pulled the comic from under my pillow and passed it across to Eileen, even though I hadn't finished reading it myself.

'And the hat out of your locker.'

For a few weeks now, I had managed to hold on to our favourite woolly hat from the mass basket, the one with the stripes knitted into it and the big white pom-pom on top. We were always fighting over it and more than once had nearly torn it in holes from trying to pull it out of each other's hands, but although Eileen was stronger than me, I usually won the day by using bribes and threats. Eileen had grown so used to the privilege of sharing my sweets and triangles of cheese, the threat of cutting her out was usually enough to bring her around to my way of thinking. The hat in question, which now lodged permanently in my locker, was so much nicer than all the others that the nurses had come to think of it as mine and so did not take it up from me after mass.

Now, of course, to keep the secret of my night walk safe, I had to do Eileen's bidding, so I promised to give up the hat in the afternoon, as soon as I was turned over on my front and could reach down into my locker.

'Well, don't you forget,' she said.

With Eileen almost satisfied I felt that I was safe. I was still confused over the strange dream, but the feel of the floor on the soles of my feet had been real enough. I could still feel the shudders of delight at the thought of it and made up my mind that I would do it again, every night, until I had taught myself to walk freely without having to hold on to anything. There would be no harm in it, I now told myself. God would understand that I had been in bed long enough.

I felt no anxiety at all when the nurses turned back my bedclothes, and so I nearly died of the shock when one of them shrieked, '*Where in the name of God did you get those black feet!*'

'And look at this sheet!' said her companion. 'Absolutely filthy!'

Nurse McGinty was called. She came flapping along the veranda and grabbed my good leg by the ankle, staring at it in disgust. 'You've been out of bed,' she said, as if that was the first I had heard of it. 'All I can say is, I'm thunderstruck! In all my years as a nurse, I have never come across such a thing.' She slapped the sole of my foot to the rhythm of her words. 'Such deceitful behaviour! Nurse, leave this bed as it is. These feet are not to be washed until Sister Finbar has seen them.' Then, as I lay shaking under her stony gaze, she turned her fury in all directions, to include the slackness of the night nurses and the sloppiness of the girls who, for all the noise they made, still couldn't keep the floor clean. She ended up by warning all of us, 'A good shake-up is needed around here, big changes made!'

You would have thought that the whole hospital was going to be closed down because of my wickedness.

The nurses went on their way in grim silence, leaving

me unwashed and my bed unmade. For an hour or more, I felt that everyone was shunning me, in case the trouble I had caused would rub off on them. Wastras, seeing that I had not been prepared to begin the day, also passed me by. She had an air of being far too busy to be bothered by whatever was going on, but I guessed, from the thinness of her lips, that she had heard and enjoyed all the details of my disgrace. I kept my arm over my eyes so I would not have to look at anyone.

At long last I heard the jingle of keys and the familiar footfall of the Bar approaching, and that was the worst moment of all. She lifted my arm and regarded me with a questioning look. I could think of no words to say and turned my head away. Fearsome thoughts raced through my mind. Would she send me home before I was cured? That was a warning we often got from nurses who complained of reaching the end of their tether.

'The gates are not locked, you know. You can take yourself off out of here, any time you like. We won't miss you.'

We took all that with a pinch of salt, giving as good as we got.

'Well, maybe I'll go tomorrow,' we would reply. 'There's plenty of other hospitals, better than here.'

Egged on by Eileen, I joined in the banter, though in spite of all the time I had been listening to her fearless repartee, I was still inclined to take the words of grown-up people seriously. I would get a clutch of fear around my heart, if I let myself think about all the worst sights I had seen in the poor parts of Dublin and Glasthule: crippled people with huge humps on their backs and twisted, useless legs. There was one young lad I used to see around the Buildings, who was so badly deformed he had to wheel himself around on the frame of an old pram. Born like that and left to bear it. There were many like that, who had to go through life classed as cripples. Cripples! That was the worst word I ever heard. We never used it in Cappagh because we were so sure that our prayers would get us better in the end.

The Bar was not the kind to make threats, but hadn't she sent Kathleen home uncured? Kathleen would surely have been left a cripple, to spend her life in a wheelchair, if God in His infinite mercy had not seen fit to make an angel of her. Well, that was all very well for her, but I was in no hurry to become an angel. When my time came to leave Cappagh, I wanted to be putting my best foot forward, like Daddy said, and for that I was nowhere near ready.

The Bar spoke at last. 'You know what you have done, don't you? You have let me down, badly!'

'I'm sorry, Sister,' I sobbed. 'I was tempted. I thought it was Our Lady telling me to get up out of my bed and walk.'

She looked puzzled, smiled a little, and then went serious again. 'Now, have a bit of sense!' she said. 'Our Lady knows better than any of us that you could have done yourself serious damage by putting weight on your leg before it is strong enough to support you. We will all be highly delighted when the time comes to get you up, but there will be no sudden miracle about it. It takes time, as you know very well. You just have to be patient and trust in God's will. I don't know what Mr Macauley will say about this at all.'

At the mention of the doctor's name, I felt I had done something so bad that it might be that sin against the Holy Ghost for which there is no forgiveness. Why else would the matter be taken to such a high authority? It was one thing to misbehave in an everyday sort of way, like pulling the beds together after the nurses had straightened them all into line or making Eileen eat the sago and swearing on my life that I had eaten it myself. But to disobey the orders of Mr Macauley was much worse than all that, and I could not begin to imagine what my punishment would be.

The nurses showed no sympathy for my misery. As they scrubbed my feet and changed my sheets, they handled me like a piece of furniture, talking to each other with tired sighs, wishing that some decent men would come along and marry them.

'Stop crying now.' The Bar came back after giving me time to think and suffer. 'We'll forgive you this time, if you give me your word that you will never do such a foolish thing again.'

'That I may be struck dead . . .'

'Stop that now! You will die in the Lord's good time and not before.' I should have remembered that she was annoyed by oaths of any kind. She began to walk away, then, as though suddenly struck by a new line of thought, she turned back and spoke to me in her normal friendly way. 'Tell me,' she said, 'were you able to walk at all?'

'She certainly was,' Eileen chipped in. 'She went all around the top of the bed and back again.'

The Bar walked on without further comment, but she was smiling.

So the day ended on a hopeful note. There was great relief in having been forgiven by Sister Finbar, and I promised Our Lady that I would tell my sin in confession and never put my feet on the floor again without permission. But I should have known that the worst was still to come. In the middle of the night I was jerked out of a deep sleep by a voice rasping in my ear and the strange, scented breath of the night sister fanning my face.

'Wake up, child,' Sister Joan commanded. 'I have a few words to say to you.'

'Bless me, Father, for I have sinned, it is two weeks since my last confession. I have two sins to confess, Father. The first one is . . . well, I'm not sure if it is a mortal sin or a venial sin.'

'Tell me what it is, child, and I'll tell you which it is.'

'I was disobedient, Father. Very disobedient.'

'In what way were you disobedient?'

'I got out of my bed.'

'Out of bed, is it! On to the floor you mean?'

'Yes, Father.'

'Without permission, I suppose?'

'Yes, Father. It was in the middle of the night. I thought I saw Our Lady. I think I really did. Well, I don't know for sure. Anyway, she was telling me to get up and go over to her in the field, and then I had this dream that I was flying in the sky . . .'

'Wait now, wait now, you have me lost entirely. Will you start again at the beginning and just tell the sin. Leave the vision and the dream out of it.'

'I got out of my bed, Father.'

'Oh, that was disobedient all right. Do you not understand the importance of doing everything you are told by the good sisters?'

'I do, Father, but I gave into temptation. I blame myself.'

'Good. You know, of course, that when we take matters into our own hands in that way, we are offending God grievously. If we all did as we liked instead of what we are told, who knows where it would end? Sure, there would be no order at all. We all have rules to keep – I myself, Sister Finbar, even the Holy Father in Rome – all bound by rules. Do you understand me?'

'I do, Father.'

'As to whether yours was a mortal sin, well, it's not the

193

worst sin I ever came across. Not in itself, that is, but it could have led you into greater evil. Wasn't it the sin of disobedience that brought about the fall of our first parents? Although you might think that the eating of an apple was innocent enough, on the face of it. Do you see what I'm saying?'

'Yes, Father.'

'As the sapling bends, so shall it grow. We'll call it a serious venial sin, all right? And now, you said you had another one to tell?'

'I was . . . rude, Father. I don't know the right name for it.'

'Explain it to me.'

'We were having our blanket baths and Eileen hadn't a stitch on her under the blanket. While we were waiting for our turn, we were fighting over a face cloth. She thumped me, so I reached out and pulled the blanket off of her. She screamed blue murder and tried to cover her shame with her hands, but I was shouting at everyone to look at her . . .'

'Oh, that was kind of grubby behaviour for a Catholic girl.'

'Another time we were playing hospital, and I made Una turn over and show us her bum, so I could stick a knitting needle in, pretending it was an injection.'

'Tut! Tut! Tut! And you with your confirmation coming up. I'm shocked. You are never to do dirty things like that. Take Our Lady as your model and behave as you know she would. Promise me now, before I give you absolution.'

'I promise, Father.'

'And you are sorry for these, and all your sins?'

'I am, Father.'

'For your penance, say three Our Fathers, three Hail

Marys and a Hail, Holy Queen. Say them slowly and reverently, thinking about the words. Ask your Holy Mother for the grace of chastity, and then say a prayer for me.'

'I will, Father.'

And now, a good Act of Contrition.'

'Oh, my God, I am heartily sorry for having offended thee, and I detest my sins above every other evil because they displease thee, my God –'

'*Te absolvo in nomine Patris et Filius et Spiritus Sanctus.*'

'Amen.'

# THE MISSIONARIES

W E HAD NO worries about meeting the archbishop, even though Wastras seemed to think
it was something to be nervous about.

'Sure, we met one before,' we reminded her. 'Well, a
bishop anyway, and the day he came to see us was as good
as a pantomime.'

'That was different,' she said, but she couldn't stop
herself from smiling with us at the memory. It was the
time when Father Alo, a Holy Ghost father who was a
friend of my family, was about to go away to the African
Missions. On hearing that I was in hospital, he came out
on an unexpected visit and being a priest was allowed in,
even though it was not a visiting day. He had with him
another priest, a gorgeous-looking fellow, all the nurses
said, who had gone to Africa soon after his ordination
and, only a few years later, was returning as a bishop for
a short visit to Ireland. Probably the youngest bishop in
the world. His diocese, we were told, covered a huge area
of Nigeria, bigger than the whole of Ireland and England
put together. But that knowledge only came later, after
some of the staff had made right fools of themselves by
not taking him seriously, although they could hardly be
blamed, for even in the eyes of the children, both priests
had all the appearances of a couple of carefree lads out
to enjoy themselves. They were so full of beans that no

one believed it when Father Alo, with a big smile, made the introductions.

'Meet the bishop!'

Wastras had laughed and slapped away the hand that was offered for her to kiss. 'Get along out of that,' she said, 'and don't be pulling our legs.' When she saw the ring she went all red and didn't know where to put herself, and weren't we only delighted to see her so embarrassed!

The priests had greatly enjoyed the joke. They stayed with us for the whole afternoon, talking about the great work they were called to do, chatting to the patients, enquiring about their progress and their families, showing not a speck of favouritism. You could see that everyone was of equal importance to them as they scooted around, answering calls from every direction.

'Father, Father, come over here – come to my bed, ah please!

'Listen till I tell you this joke.'

'Do you know this song?'

And the stories the bishop had to tell! My God, you would hardly believe what wonderful Catholics some of those poor black people became, who had never even heard of Jesus and Mary until the White Fathers came and taught them how to save their souls. Some of them even became priests and nuns. He told us that to his parishioners walking twenty miles to hear mass was nothing, even if it took a day and a night to reach the mission, for they had no transport only their feet. Mass would be said for them on whatever day they arrived, for they couldn't always make it for Sundays. We listened in amazement to tales of terrible hardship that we, in the safety of Ireland, would not be able to endure and how, when they caught incurable diseases or their babies died, those people were able to accept without question or complaint that it was all part of God's plan, and, of course, the one thing they were never short of was babies.

At teatime, the bishop put a nurse's veil on his head and did the rounds with the trolley, while Father Alo gave out bread and cake as if he had been doing it all his life. Nurse McGinty said that if they ever got fed up with the foreign missions, there would be jobs for them in Cappagh.

The afternoon had been one long laugh for us, and on the whole length of the veranda, there wasn't a soul who was not cheered up by the antics of the two wonderful visitors. When it came to an end, they stood together at a spot between the two wards, the smiles wiped off their faces as with bowed heads they offered prayers, first for the children of Cappagh and all those who had care of them, then for the propagation of the faith on the continent of Africa. With great sweeps of their arms, they gave us their blessings and, as parting gifts, handed out printed cards bearing their photographs and a request to be included in our daily prayers, to help them in the immense task that was entrusted to them. As they left the hospital, they were all smiles again, saying without a trace of regret that they would not see Ireland again for another eight years.

We loved to recall the memory of that visit which, for a short while at least, filled some of us with religious vocations. Eileen, Pauline and I made up our minds that as soon as we were old enough and cured of our afflictions we would become nuns and go out to Africa. We would dedicate our lives to working alongside the White Fathers, saving the black babies from having to go to limbo for all eternity, and while we were at it, being certain sure of saving our own souls. The idea soon faded, but we never forgot the way the light of Christ had shone out of the faces of the two missionaries as they talked about Africa. You would have thought that out there was heaven itself.

But in the matter of our approaching confirmation, Wastras said we were to put all that frivolity out of our minds. The Archbishop of Dublin was a different kettle of fish altogether. A man of great power and wisdom, he was to be shown the utmost respect on his visit, which would not be sociable in any way but an occasion of great solemnity. He was coming to confer the sacrament of confirmation on the children of his diocese – that was to say, all those who were worthy of such an honour. As long as he was in the hospital, she said, we were to be on our best behaviour, speaking only when spoken to, answering any questions he might ask, clearly and without mumbling or drawing attention to ourselves in any way.

It went without saying, of course, that we all had to be in the state of grace. There was another anxiety, for even though we went to confession regularly and were used to examining our consciences, there was always the chance that some little sin might have slipped our minds.

# CONFIRMATION

IN OUR CONFIRMATION garments we felt beautiful and pure of heart. Even our flawed bodies made us feel proud on that day, for we were left in no doubt that our suffering, in all its forms, had brought us closer to God.

Keeping still, so as not to disturb the folds of our finery, we waited in joyful expectation for the coming of the Archbishop of Dublin. We, the privileged ones, were placed evenly along a cleared space on the veranda. All the other beds were pushed well down to each end, giving us pride of place. Just as on that other great day, when we made our first Holy Communion, our beds were festooned with white veiling, silk bows and waxen flowers. Around our necks we wore medals hung on blue ribbons, specially engraved to mark the occasion of our becoming strong and perfect Christians. These medals, Sister Patrick had told us, we must keep as cherished possessions, for they had been personally blessed by the archbishop, who in turn had kissed the hand of our Holy Father, the pope.

Between each bed, an up-patient sat on a straight chair. Keeping still was harder for them, but no one complained. Comfort was of small importance on such a day.

Now that we had been fully prepared and cleansed of our sins, we should have been free of all worry, but the

200

anxiety still remained that we might be asked a question that we could not answer. What would the archbishop do then, we wondered? Have us pulled out of the line maybe and left at the back of the ward until it was all over? The catechism was not easy to learn by heart. I for one still could not tell the difference between consanguinity and affinity, even after all the weeks of Sister Patrick's patient teaching.

On either side of me, Pauline and Eileen, too, were aglow with pride and joy. Beyond them, standing out among the Little Flowers, with her veil pulled forward to hide her purple cheek, even Ann Kelly looked better than you could ever imagine. She was so quiet, anyone who didn't know her would think that butter wouldn't melt in her mouth. Was she in the state of grace, I couldn't help wondering? By the looks of her, I guessed that she had made a firm resolution to give up her loud, ignorant ways.

Sister Finbar and Sister de Montford were dressed in Sunday black, their faces still and solemn as they kept watch on the gate. Nurse McGinty's was the only moving figure in the scene. She paraded slowly up and down with folded arms, looking for the slightest flaw in the cleaning operations which had been going on for days past, even though she knew perfectly well that there was not a crumb or a speck of dirt to be found anywhere on the scrubbed and polished floors.

Suddenly, the silence was fractured by a hoarse cry from Ann Kelly, who was first to see the flashing of car roofs skimming along the top of the driveway hedge. She tried to shout quietly, the way you would in a church, to show reverence, but was quickly overtaken by the excitement of the moment, and her voice rose to the roar of a street gurrier selling newspapers.

'HERE 'EE IS – THE ARCH-A-BISHOP! LOOK AT ALL THEM CARS!'

'Quiet!' someone barked. 'Will someone tell that girl to keep her voice down!'

Wastras, looking desperate, stepped forward and raised her lilting voice, chopping the air with her arms to start us all singing the opening hymn:

*Holy God, we praise thy name,*
*Lord of all, we bow before thee.*

The limousines halted at the top of the drive. We heard the heavy closing of car doors and moments later, through the open gates, a horde of acolytes broke through, their surplices flapping like the sails of yachts in a strong breeze. At first they seemed to move in an aimless way, scudding about in the space between the altar and the verandas, then suddenly in their midst appeared the towering golden figure that was, without a doubt, His Grace, the Archbishop of Dublin. The trees swayed and the sun broke out of a mountainous cloud, catching the facets of his bejewelled vestments so that he sparkled as he moved and we could hardly keep our eyes on him without squinting.

With measured steps he made his way towards Saint Joseph's veranda. Calmly now, his attendants fell into a double column behind him. Censers were swung, and before long the fragrance of holy incense reached our nostrils. Strong, priestly voices were added to those of the children and the squawking crows, in a great swell of invocation:

*Come, O Creator Spirit blest, and in our souls take up*
*thy rest.*
*Come with thy grace and heavenly aid, to fill the hearts*
*which thou has made.*

We watched the rise and fall of His Grace's hand and the movements of his mitred head as he made his way slowly along the beds of Saint Joseph's with his shepherd's crook, blessing all before him. When the big Johnnies were all done, he walked swiftly past the little lads of Saint Michael's and disappeared for a short time into the babies' ward. Then he came bursting on to our veranda and we were in his presence at last. Nuns and nurses dipped a knee and kissed his great amethyst ring as he lowered his hand from the blessings. As he turned his face towards us, his smile was thin and his eyes remote, as if his gaze could not quite reach us but was importantly occupied with something hovering in the space between.

'Rosemary, Joan, Elizabeth.' His Grace repeated the names muttered into his ear by his serving priest, reading from a list. He pronounced the Latin words of the sacrament and called the Holy Spirit down upon me. He anointed my forehead with sweet smelling holy oil, laid his long, white hand briefly on my cheek, and it was done. My nervousness melted away and I promised in my head to accept any cross, any danger or persecution which the Lord saw fit to send me. Nothing, I vowed, would ever shake my faith, my whole life long. Then the great man spoke to me personally, and to my great surprise his voice was as homely as Sister Finbar's on a good day.

'Tell me now,' he said, 'what do you want to be when you are grown up?'

'A saint, Your Grace,' I answered, quick as a flash.

He nodded his head approvingly. 'That's the good girl,' he said, and all around my bed faces broke into broad smiles. Then he waved his arm and raised his voice to include us all. 'Now, will you all say together, "Hail, Holy Queen . . ."'

The feasting and congratulating went on all day. We had presents, mostly of the religious variety, showered upon us by nurses and girls, every one of them bursting with emotion at the sight of us. Nuns that we hardly knew came down from the convent, and we were told that some of the Finglas people had left in bags of biscuits and sweets for us at the convent door, as if, Nurse McGinty laughed, we weren't getting properly fed.

'You are all beautiful,' we were told many times. 'Anything you pray for today will surely be granted.'

When evening came, we were still full of excitement and could not sleep. Long after dark, we were still talking about the events of the day.

'Wasn't he a wonderful man, that arch-a-bishop?'

'But a bit pale, though, very white and serious looking.'

'And sad, too, with his long, thin face. Sister Patrick says the burden of his responsibilities lies heavy on his shoulders.'

'We must pray for him so.'

We sighed over our long list of people we had to pray for and were only too happy to agree when Eileen said, 'We'll just say the one prayer, really well, and let that do for the lot of them.'

We joined our hands and said again the prayer that had brought us all the praise: 'Hail, Holy Queen, Mother of Mercy. Hail our life, our sweetness and our hope . . .' speaking the words with pride, as if we had made them up ourselves.

As soon as we said 'Amen,' Pauline, who always seemed to think of something more to say just when Eileen and I were ready for sleep, spoke into the dark.

'Mind you, I didn't see his dear face at all. I seen the golden robes of him and the sparkles as he came through the gates, but when he came close and put his hand on my head, all I could smell was lilies – you know, that perfume you get when someone dies – so I kept my eyes closed the whole time, like when I'm receivin' Holy Communion . . .' She interrupted herself to give out one of her sermons. 'Don't you know, Eileen, that you should always keep your eyes closed when you're receivin' a sacrament?'

Eileen gave another deep sigh. 'God, 'ou're an awful drip. Didn't 'ou miss the best part! He was real friendly. I had a good look at him and gave him a smile – and he smiled back.'

'He did not!'

'He did so. Cross my heart and hope to . . .'

I threw my comfort blanket over my head and left them arguing.

'Do you know what, Mummy . . . I answered my question perfectly and the archbishop was delighted with me. All the priests were smiling. I said the whole prayer straight through without a hitch. We had our photograph taken, too, so if it comes out you will see for yourself what a great day it was. Oh, Mummy, you would have loved to be there. Amen. (Sorry, I forgot to say 'how are you' and send my best wishes to the baby.)'

Coming back to the veranda, I asked aloud, 'I wonder why this world is called the "valley of tears?"' But there was no one still awake to give thought to the question.

# Last Days

SURE ENOUGH, THE Holy Ghost had not come empty-handed but filled us to overflowing with all those cardinal virtues promised by Sister Patrick: charity, joy, peace and patience – and others, too, long words which we never understood but in any case, would not be needing until later on in our lives. In the grip of so much fervour, we crossed our hearts and swore never again to be rude or fall out with each other.

For myself, I was not a bit surprised when, only a short while later, Mr Macauley decided the time had come to try me out on my feet. 'A calliper won't do for the hip,' he said, talking to Sister Finbar over my head, 'but maybe a plaster cast, and yes, I don't see why she shouldn't have shoes.'

'The mother would prefer shoes.'

'Of course, she would,' said the doctor.

And so my feet were measured and new shoes sent for. Daddy brought them the very next Sunday, wrapped in tissue paper and nestling in a cardboard box with 'Bradley's' written on the lid. I kept them in bed beside me, all the time taking them out for another look, smelling the leather, untying the laces and doing them up again.

So great was this miracle that all the hardship was taken out of an afternoon spent in the plaster room with a team of light-hearted nurses who sang as they went about their messy work. I sang along with them as they bandaged my body from the waist and down the bad leg as far as the knee. I lay naked on a steel table, cold and wet as they slapped and smoothed on the plaster, assuring me that with all the stray splashes that were made, my modesty was well preserved. 'You might as well be wearing big white bloomers!' they assured me.

When they had finished, my body and half a leg were safe inside a cast, which one nurse said was as thick as the wall of a white-washed cottage. There was even a window, she joked as she smoothed the edges of the hole, for I still had a deep wound in my thigh, which had to be painted and dressed every day. Lastly, with a copy-ink pencil, they wrote the date large across the front of the cast and sent me out to dry on the veranda.

The day those shoes were put on my feet was the best day of my life, and I knew that as long as I lived I would never forget the feel of them or the pride I felt in owning them. They gave me protection and the courage, first to stand beside my bed and, soon after, to walk without fear. Within a few days I was able to cross the width of the ward without assistance and go visiting all the beds on Blessed Imelda's veranda.

Of the three of us, only Eileen was still a bed-patient, but she said she wasn't too bothered about that. She was on a reversed spinal frame every day now and could hang out of her bed and reach for things. 'Just like a monkey,' Nurse McGinty said whenever she caught her out.

'Don't be worryin' about me at all,' Eileen said in a superior way. 'I'm not goin' home just yet, but haven't my prayers been answered in a different way that will keep me happy while I'm waitin'?'

With her head and chest raised high, she leaned on

her elbows and stretched her neck to gaze towards the
spot on the Little Flower's veranda, where she would
soon find herself in what she called 'the very best of company'. She would be moved, Sister Finbar said, as soon as
Pauline and myself were discharged from the hospital.
Almost from the moment she heard the news, Eileen
took to shouting up to the Biddy she most admired. 'Can
'ou hear me, Ann? Hey, Ann Kelly!'

'I hear ya!' came the reply. 'Who are ya?'

'Eileen – Eileen Cassidy – C-AH-S-S-I-D-Y.

'OK, Eileen Cassidy. What ya want with me?'

'I'm ten years old and I'm comin' up tomorrow. Can
I be beside 'ou?'

During a long pause, Eileen called out 'ple-ase' once
or twice and, 'I'll bring all my comics.'

At last a reply came. 'If ya know how to behave yerself!'
This was followed by a piercing whistle, which Eileen took
to be a sign of acceptance. She tried to whistle back, but
she hadn't quite got the knack of it, so she could hardly
manage a sound at all. Instead, she continued to shout
and wave her arms in the air until I put my hands over my
ears and told her to be quiet. Eileen scribbled notes,
which she begged the girls to deliver. 'Ann Kelly is my
new friend,' she said proudly. 'There'll be no more
child's play for me.'

On our last day together, we sat one on either side of
Eileen's bed, not talking much, each of us thinking about
our separate futures. We were cutting out paper dolls
from a book provided by Sister Finbar to keep us busy
while we waited for the ambulance to come for me. The
rosy-cheeked dolls, two of them, stood side by side on the
cover of the book, one dark and one fair – Snow White
and Rose Red, we called them. Chunky, healthy-looking
girls they were, with dimples in their knees. Inside the

book were pages of stylish clothes: party frocks, tennis
and swimming outfits, hats and nightdresses, everything
you would expect to find in a grand trousseau. These two
dolls, I thought, had the kind of life that I was looking
forward to myself, with clothes for every occasion, but I
kept this thought to myself, knowing that my two com-
panions would never be so lucky. Once or twice I wondered about the lives they would have after leaving
Cappagh, and even though their faces showed trust and
contentment, I still felt sorry for them. I cut carefully
around the dotted lines of the dolls' clothes and passed
each garment across to Pauline. She received each one
with wide-eyed expressions of admiration – or disap-
proval – for the kind of style that had no meaning for her,
as she hung them laboriously by their slits and tabs over
the shoulders of the dolls.

My own dress was what Mammy called the colour of
buttercups, patterned with shapes like teardrops. I
paused often in the cutting out to brush away the slivers
of paper that fell into my lap, taking pleasure from the
thought that I would be gone before the girls came on in
the morning and discovered the mess on the floor. The
material felt soft under my hand, and I announced to all
those who would listen, 'This pattern is called paisley, and
the material is of the very best of quality.'

'You told us that a hundred times,' said Eileen, without even looking.

Pauline gazed at the dress with a puzzled expression.
'I'm not sayin' it's awful,' she said, 'though I'd have gone
for blue meself, something with flowers on it, and maybe
a bit o' lace.'

'My other dress is blue,' I told her, smoothing the skirt
down to cover my plaster cast. I stretched out my feet to
admire my laced-up shoes and sparkling white ankle

socks. As long as I kept my feet close together, the block of leather on the sole of the right shoe could not be seen from above.

I had been ready to go home since early morning, and the day felt as long as a week. My thoughts reached out towards tomorrow when, if the weather was good, I might stroll along the seafront with Mummy and my little sister. I could see it all! I would be wearing the blue dress for a change and would be pushing the pram, and the people of Sandycove would turn out in large numbers to welcome me home.

I grew tired of sitting so awkwardly on the chair, with the plastered leg hanging down the side. At times I wished I could lie down and go to sleep, to wake up just as the ambulance arrived, but then again I wanted to be the first to see it coming through the gates. Anyway, I had to stay where I was, for the bed was no longer mine to use as I pleased. It had been stripped down, the waterproof mattress had been scrubbed and a pile of clean sheets placed on it, ready to be made up for a new patient who, the nurses said, would not be long arriving. The locker, too, was empty, my belongings packed in a cardboard carton which stood near me on the floor. Marjorie and Teresa lay side by side on the top, asleep under a doll's blanket.

'I'll be gettin' a box like that when I go to the convalescent home,' Pauline told us, also repeating herself for the third or fourth time. 'It's a happy place, you know, more like a home than a hospital. Sometimes they take you out for a day to the seaside. After I've been there a while, I might get sent to another place, where I'll be taught easy work and . . . I'm not sure yet but . . .' Her voice faded away for want of certain knowledge.

She was silent for a while, as though giving all her

attention to the paper dolls. Then she clicked her tongue a few times and shaking her head from side to side murmured, hardly above a whisper, 'Only . . . I'll surely be lonely for ye all and Sister Finbar.'

On hearing those words, hot tears rolled slowly down my cheeks, and for a few moments I allowed myself to think that it would be no bad thing to stay in Cappagh for a little while longer. It would be fun to go up the veranda with Eileen – for a day or two only, just to get the feel of being a Little Flower. I would also enjoy going with Pauline on her afternoon walks down to see the babies. Once having found my feet, I might even venture across to the far side of the altar, to have a look at the field where the nurses played camogie, and look back at the wards with the eyes of a visitor coming through the gates. I might even go in search of my Johnny's bed on Saint Joseph's veranda. Just to wave. I thought about him often and would have loved to say goodbye and get another wink from him.

But I was going home. Almost as soon as my plaster was dry, the decision had been made. 'There are some that we wouldn't let go so soon,' Sister Finbar and the doctor agreed, 'but this child comes from a good family who will take proper care of her.' Smiling down on me she added, 'We are all delighted.'

There was nothing in the world to be sad about, and yet more tears came. Nurse McGinty lifted me on to the unmade mattress and loosened my shoelaces, in case my shoes were beginning to pinch a bit. 'You are just over-tired,' she said.

The scissors dropped from my hand and the cutting-out book slid to the floor. I lifted my hands to my hot cheeks. 'This is the happiest day of my life,' I said. 'In about one hour from now I'll be at home in our dining room, eating strawberries and cake.' In my mind's eye I saw Mummy, mashing the luscious berries in a bowl, pouring in lashings of cream and sugar, the way she used to long ago. 'I like them with bread and butter,' she'd say as she smeared the butter thickly on a pan loaf and shaved off wafer-thin slices, laughing as we all chanted together, 'Do have a bit of bread on your butter.'

'Quick, Nurse – the bowl! I'm going to be sick!'

Too late. Lumps of carrot and unchewed meat shot out of my mouth and across the floor, destroying the perfection of my new clothes with jagged splashes of bile, like the droppings of crows.

Evening crept along the veranda. The sun fell suddenly down behind the convent. Shouts became murmurs, restless movements slowed down, then ceased. Bored now with the cut-outs, we turned our attention to a pile of old comics that we had read many times before, the best that could be found in Eileen's locker. In the fading light we read them yet again, holding them close to our screwed-up eyes. Pauline was put to bed, Eileen turned over on her back for the night. Night nurses began to arrive. They laughed when they saw me. 'Is it still here you are! Have we to say goodbye to you all over again?' They stopped in their tracks when they saw Sister Finbar still on duty and in bad humour.

'I can't think what is keeping the ambulance,' she kept saying, reaching into the mysterious depths of her habit for another look at her pocket watch. 'I'll just go and telephone again. Drink your water now, 'twill settle your stomach.'

I sipped obediently while Eileen yawned and Pauline fed her pearly beads through her fingers. Sister Finbar returned with a parting gift from Saint Anthony's, a boy doll made of celluloid. I knew he was meant to be a boy because he was dressed in a hand knitted romper suit. I at once named him 'Philip' – the name that Mummy would have chosen if our baby had been a boy. I kissed my new child fondly and laid him down to sleep between his sisters. 'I'll play with you when I get home,' I said.

The ambulance came noisily through the gates, its headlamps dim and short-sighted. Stern-faced, Sister Finbar, a white, flapping figure in the twilight, with two red spots of anger in her cheeks, stepped out to beckon it towards us. Two attendants approached her and touched their caps, telling a complicated story. They were given the wrong instructions . . . only late in the day . . . they had been sent to the wrong hospital . . . it was not their fault. It was a disgrace, Sister Finbar told them, she would complain.

Turning to us again, she spread her arms wide over our heads. 'Shake hands now, the three of you,' she said. 'You have been together a long time.'

From somewhere in the gloaming a shout went up:

'*Three cheers for Rosemary: Hip, Hip, Hip!*'

Blankets moved and heads rose up to answer the call. '*Hooray! Hooray! Hooray!*' Voices rang out, the full length of every veranda and came back to me in uneven echoes that repeated themselves endlessly inside my head.

'*Hooray! Hooray! Hooray!*'

Quietly we spoke our goodbyes – Eileen, Pauline and myself, Rosemary, no longer in the middle. As our hands met limply, our eyes dropped downwards in sudden shyness.

'You will meet again, please God,' Sister Finbar said. 'You will be back to see us for the clinics and the change of plaster. This is not the end.'

The two men helped me to my feet and guided me

towards the open doors of the ambulance, raising me high as they offered me up to my great reward.

## SOME OTHER READING

*from*

## BRANDON

Brandon is a leading Irish publisher of new fiction and non-fiction for an international readership. For a catalogue of new and forthcoming books, please write to Brandon/Mount Eagle, Cooleen, Dingle, Co. Kerry, Ireland. For a full listing of all our books in print, please go to

www.brandonbooks.com

# LILY O'CONNOR

*Can Lily O'Shea Come Out to Play?*

A bestseller in Ireland and Australia, a fascinating story of growing up Protestant in Dublin.

This vivid memoir of a childhood in the 1930s and '40s is marked by its narrator's consciousness of her status as an outsider, for Lily is a child of a mixed marriage, baptised a Protestant but living in a Catholic community. The originality of this account of a working-class childhood is its portrait of a spirited girl coming to terms with her difference. At its heart this is a universal story of childhood; of hardship and joy, of violence, poverty, pleasure, humour and, over all, humanity.

"Anyone with half an interest in times gone by will enjoy this well-written anecdotal book." *Irish Criticism*

"A vibrant recollection of childhood, this – honest, warm and often moving." *Examiner*

ISBN 0 86322 267 6; Paperback

# ALICE
# TAYLOR

To School
Through the Fields

AN INTERNATIONAL BESTSELLER

## ALICE TAYLOR

### *To School Through the Fields*

"One of the most richly evocative and moving portraits of childhood [ever] written . . . A journey every reader will treasure and will want to read over and over again."
*Boston Herald*

ISBN 0 86322 099 1; Paperback

### *Quench the Lamp*

"She has a writer's eye and instinct and the world of her girlhood, which is evoked in this book, is fully realised, palpable . . . The world that she is writing about has all but disappeared, and I think that we are all in Ms Taylor's debt for having chronicled it for us with such simplicity and grace." *Irish Independent*

ISBN0 86322 112 2; Paperback

### *The Village*

"What makes the story unique is Taylor's disarming style; she writes as though she were sitting next to you, at dusk, recounting the events of her week . . . Taylor has a knack for finding the universal truth in daily details."
*Los Angeles Times*

ISBN 0 86322 142 4; Paperback

## The Woman
## of the House
HER NUMBER 1 BESTSELLING NOVEL

# ALICE TAYLOR

## *Country Days*

"A rich patchwork of tales and reminiscences by the bestselling village postmistress from Co. Cork. Alice Taylor is a natural writer." *Daily Telegraph*

ISBN 0 86322 168 8; Paperback

## *The Woman of the House*

"This well-crafted novel explores the mixed fortunes of the residents in an Irish village. Taylor skilfully shows the intricacies of country life and the strong tide of emotions which flows under the most placid of exteriors."
*Belfast Telegraph*

ISBN 0 86322 249 8; Paperback

## *Across the River*

"Alice Taylor is an outstanding storyteller. Like a true seanchaí, she uses detail to signal twists in the plot or trouble ahead . . . It is tightly plotted fiction, an old-fashioned page-turner." *The Irish Times*

ISBN 0 86322 285 4; Paperback

# Wilson John Haire
## *The Yard*

Wilson John Haire entered the Belfast shipyard as an office boy at fourteen. Brought up mainly in rural areas, he was suddenly thrown into the world's biggest shipyard, a huge cauldron of twisted metal, great baulks of timber, the freezing sea, death and terrible injuries.

"A true eye-opener for younger, cossetted generations, which is also sure to trigger bitter-sweet memories for older readers. A well-crafted, clever and gripping account."
*News Letter* (Belfast)

"He writes very, very well. He's got a way of bringing alive a whole range of characters. There's a grinding poverty here but there's also a kind of resilience. I would recommend this." *Rattlebag, RTE Radio One*

"His mordant, humorous account of Belfast life smacks of Dickens, and the stories are told in a snappy and evocative style with a playwright's timing." *Camden New Journal*

"The style is of gritty realism – writing with no room for sentiment, but which contains a bleak beauty all its own . . . compelling." *Belfast Telegraph*

ISBN 0 86322 296 X; Paperback

# Kitty Fitzgerald

## *Snapdragons*

"*Snapdragons* is a rattling one-sit read, rich with Irish rhythms and laced with a wonderfully bitter and witty ongoing dialogue between the heroine Bernice and her cantankerous, wheedling God. The early, Irish part of the novel is a powerful evocation of a godfearing rural community which reveals itself to be every bit as cruel as the seedy Birmingham underworld to which the girls escape." *Northern Review*

"Startling, humorous, light of touch." *Books Ireland*

"A unique and extremely engaging rites of passage novel set in post-war Birmingham, centred around the difficult relationship between two sisters, each looking for love and salvation in their different ways. It combines realism with warmth and humour." *Irish Post*

ISBN 0 86322 258 7; Paperback

# MARIE McGANN

## *The Drawbridge*

"Marie McGann is a real find. She writes with the exhilaration and defiance of youth and the wisdom of age. A moving and triumphant novel." *Fay Weldon*

"*The Drawbridge* is an assured debut, offering no pat answers . . . At its heart [it] is about love in its many forms, and the struggle to throw off the shackles of defensiveness and self preservation and at last attain the freedom to love without fear." *Sunday Tribune*

"This is a first novel with the kind of story established writers would die to produce . . . A page-turner, a delight, a revelation . . . I loved this one." *IT*

ISBN 0 86322 271 4; Paperback

# JENNIFER CHAPMAN

## *Jeremy's Baby*

"A page-turning tale of contemporary mores."
*Rosemary Friedman*

"Set against a backdrop of Aga cookery, weekend lunches in
the country, arts review programmes on television, it's also a
novel about birth and death, love and jealousy, friendship
and betrayal . . . But it's in the development of the characters,
and in the author's near-scientific fascination with the
workings of their minds, that the book's strength lies."
*Sunday Tribune*

"Anything Jennifer Chapman writes must be taken seriously."
*The Times*

ISBN  0 86322 277 3; Paperback